LET IT SHINE!

Let It Shine!

THE EMERGENCE OF AFRICAN AMERICAN
CATHOLIC WORSHIP

Mary E. McGann, R.S.C.J.

WITH CONTRIBUTIONS BY
Eva Marie Lumas, S.S.S., and Ronald D. Harbor

FORDHAM UNIVERSITY PRESS   NEW YORK   2008

Another version of Part One appeared in *U.S. Catholic Historian* 2, no.10 (Spring 2001): 27–65; used with permission. Another version of Part Two appeared in *Worship* 76, no.1 (January 2002): 2–24; used with permission. Another version of Part Three appeared in "Constructing an African American Catholic Aesthetic: Ways and Means of Negotiating the Amens in the Liturgical Assembly"; unpublished M.T.S. Thesis, Franciscan School of Theology, 2001; used with permission.

Library of Congress Cataloging-in-Publication Data

McGann, Mary E.
    Let it shine! : the emergence of African American Catholic worship / edited by Mary E. McGann with contributions by Eva Marie Lumas and Ronald D. Harbor.—1st ed.

        p.   cm.
    Includes bibliographical references (p.) and index.
    ISBN 978–0-8232–2991–8 (cloth : alk. paper)—
    ISBN 978–0-8232–2992–5 (pbk. : alk. paper)
        1. African American Catholics—Religious life—History—20th century.
    2. Catholic Church—United States—Liturgy—History—20th century.   I. Lumas, Eva Marie.   II. Harbor, Ronald D.   III. Title.
    BX1407.N4M337   2008
    264″.02008996073—dc22

                                                                        2008020226

Printed in the United States of America
10 09 08   5 4 3 2 1
First edition

CONTENTS

INTRODUCTION   ix

PART ONE: AN HISTORICAL OVERVIEW
The Emergence of African American Catholic Worship
MARY E. MCGANN, R.S.C.J., AND EVA MARIE LUMAS, S.S.S.   1

PART TWO: FOUNDATIONAL VISION
Clarence R. J. Rivers' Vision of Effective African American Worship
MARY E. MCGANN, R.S.C.J.   53

PART THREE: AESTHETIC PRINCIPLES
Constructing an African American Catholic Liturgical Aesthetic
RONALD D. HARBOR   85

A FINAL TRIBUTE   133

NOTES   137
SELECT BIBLIOGRAPHY   165
CONTRIBUTORS   173
INDEX   175

This little light of mine, I'm gonna let it shine!
This little light of mine, I'm gonna let it shine!
This little light of mine, I'm gonna let it shine!
Let it shine! Let it shine! Let it shine!

Jesus gave it to me. I'm gonna let it shine! . . .

All over the world, I'm gonna let it shine! . . .

This song pays homage to the ongoing strivings of the African American Catholic community to articulate its distinctive ethno-religiosity as a people who are at once Black and Catholic. Within that process, no pastoral interest has received the density of reflection, innovation, and debate as the topic of worship. This volume chronicles the forty-year apex of that journey. It probes the distinctive contribution Black Catholics have made to the worship life of the American Church and thus to the historical unfolding of lived Christianity in the United States.

Beginning with the 1960s—a *kairos* time for Black Catholics brought about through the convergence of Vatican Council II and the Civil Rights movement—the authors of this volume explore the powerful renaissance that has marked African American self-understandings over the last several decades by examining one critical dimension: the forging of new expressions of Catholic worship, at once rooted in the larger Catholic tradition and shaped by the aesthetic predilections and theological presuppositions that flow from the wellsprings of African American religious culture.

Let It Shine! is situated within four intersecting conversations. First, a focus on the cultural complexity of the U.S. Catholic Church has marked a whole spectrum of theological and pastoral writing over the past few years, and with it a closer attention to the concrete forms, expressions, and ritual embodiments by which particular cultural communities express their Christian faith. The essays of this volume are a unique inquiry into the experience of African American Catholics at a defining moment in their faith journey. Through the lens of emerging liturgical practice, the authors explore the interplay of cultural consciousness, religious sensibilities, local agency, and charismatic leadership that has shaped distinctively new expressions of Catholic faith. What becomes clear in this ferment is that to be "Black and Catholic" is a deliberate choice—a way of living authentically the catholicity of their shared faith tradition and of being agents of their future, subjects of their full participation in the Church. While Black Catholics are neither monolithic nor uniform in their responses, critiques, starting points, or religious sensibilities, the process of setting in motion new forms of liturgical practice has brought about a contemporary articulation of African American Catholic faith, life, and culture that is unmatched by earlier generations, and that had remained mostly implicit in previous centuries.

Second, "lived religion" is of increasing interest in many fields of study, including theology, religious studies, and Church history, and with it a focus on "practice."[1] Practice can be understood as "those things Christian people do together, over time, to address fundamental human needs in response to and in light of God's active presence."[2] Practice is a way people actualize their faith and negotiate their passage within a larger tradition. It is lived and concrete, while always remaining fluid, flexible, and adaptive to changing circumstances.[3]

The essays of this volume explore one aspect of Black Catholic practice—namely worship—and document the social change, cultural awakening, and ritual resourcefulness that have energized its evolving shape over the past few decades. In so doing, they bring to light the pivotal role that liturgical practice has played: first, as a site for the construction of new expressions of embodied theology and spirituality; and second, as a matrix for negotiating the intersecting boundaries of what it means to be *both* African and American, *both* Black and Catholic. This "hybrid" religious identity[4]—which Black scholar W. E. B. Du Bois, writing in the early twentieth century, referred to as a "double consciousness"[5]—has been an intrinsic part of the collective history of African Americans. But it has been evoked in new ways in this realm of concrete worship practice, and has released generative forces that have renegotiated the porous boundaries between Blackness and Catholicity, while at the same time rooting African American Catholics more deeply in both worlds.[6] What is learned within this crucible of practice is that hybridity is most fruitful when boundaries are not collapsed but remain in creative tension.[7]

Third, most assessments of the impact of the liturgical reforms of Vatican II on lived practice in the American Church have been done from the perspective of white Catholic communities.[8] Moreover, they have focused primarily on ritual adaptation and its relationship to Church life. A considerably different narrative emerges when viewed from the perspective of the Church's cultural complexity and pluralistic practice. Indeed, more radical change has taken place within communities whose cultural expressions were historically excluded from Catholic worship through persistent racism and systematic cultural hegemony.

Let It Shine! brings to light the remarkable transformation and change that has marked the practice of African American communities across the United States, identifying the cultural intuitions and sacramental sensibilities that have shaped their renewed expression of Catholic liturgy. This alternative narrative reveals that liturgical renewal is inseparable from social change; that inculturation and liberation go hand and hand;[9] that renewal and revolution are mutually invigorating; and that theology and worship are forged in a common search for right living before God. It confirms that ecclesial processes of renewal are never simply top-down, or from the center to the margins. Rather they are a dialogic interplay of regulation and custom, of normativity and improvisation, of directives and resistance.[10] Agency has been critical for Black Catholics—the empowerment to name and claim their place in the larger Church and to shape their own future.[11] In contrast to the circumspect logic of liturgical renewal set in motion in many places, the forging of distinctive styles and patterns of African American Catholic worship has released a religious energy and desire, a giftedness and grace, a boldness and passion, that continues to follow its own logic in an attempt to find its appropriate and legitimate course.

Fourth, in this first decade of a new millennium, liturgy has resurfaced as an urgent pastoral concern within the African American Catholic community. Unlike the decades documented in this volume, there is currently no forum, no central office or nationally acknowledged leadership to guide African American communities through the complexities of emerging liturgical rubrics, divergent episcopal preferences, and staid or uncritically adapted parish liturgical practices, while at the same time honoring the spiritual sensibilities of Black Catholics. Meeting in the summer of 2006, African American pastoral leaders called for a focused effort to gather the experience and insight of Black bishops, theologians, parish leaders, liturgical innovators, scholars, and "people from the pew" to identify those liturgical practices that best inform, express, and give meaning to their faith in these times.[12] Such a comprehensive effort is necessary, they contend, if African American Catholic worship is to claim its historical inheritance and realize the fullness of its emerging potential.

Let It Shine! provides a cogent summary of the significant insights and pastoral initiatives that should not be forgotten or misrepresented in a deliberation of such importance. Hence it offers the African American Catholic community an invaluable resource—a conceptual framework for an appreciative inquiry into the legacy and future of its liturgical prayer traditions. At a time when the Black community is increasingly dispersed geographically, culturally isolated, and religiously eclectic, such a framework can guide the continued articulation of the spiritual genius of Black Catholics, building on the dynamic ferment of the period covered in this volume while creating its own new paths and tributaries.

Set within these intersecting conversations, Part One provides an historical overview of the emergence of Black Catholic worship, documenting and interpreting the historical forces that served as catalyst, the prophetic leadership that guided the process, the liturgical and contextual issues that shaped the movement, and the fruits of this journey that have now been released into the larger American church. To do this, it draws on a range of resources—books, articles, media, surveys, scholarly insights from various disciplines, and conversations with persons within and beyond the Catholic Church. In concluding, authors Mary McGann and Eva Lumas address the present and future challenges that Black Catholics face as they continue their journey of faith, discerning the distinctive patterns that can express their worship of the living God in a changing social, cultural, and ecclesial context.

Part Two examines the foundational vision of Catholic worship articulated by Father Clarence R. J. Rivers in the 1970s. Rivers—at once a musician, theologian, liturgist, composer, dramatist, and priest of the diocese of Cincinnati—worked to educate and "liberate" Black Catholics to reclaim the fullness of their ethno-religious patrimony. His writings articulate an understanding of "effective" African American worship based in the sacramental sensibilities, theological premises, cultural intuitions, and ethical wisdom of Black Christianity. Building on the historical data of Part One—which documents Rivers' crucial and prophetic leadership in fueling a renaissance in Black worship, music, preaching, and prayer—author Mary McGann lays out Rivers' performative approach to Catholic liturgy, and enumerates the cultural-religious foundations on which it is based. In concluding, she notes the salience of Rivers' vision, articulated in the 1970s, for the contemporary church.

Part Three constructs a liturgical aesthetic, based on the work of four African American scholars: Bishop Edward Kenneth Braxton, Doctor Toinette Eugene, Father Glenn Jean-Marie, and Father Clarence Rivers. Contending that the theological, anthropological, ethical, and liturgical concerns of these scholars, presented to the Black Catholic Theological Symposium in 1978, remain pertinent to authentic Black worship today, author Ronald D. Harbor weaves together their insights as the basis for a Black Catholic liturgical aesthetic, expressed through twenty-three "performative values" that can guide the efforts of Black Catholic communities now and into the future. Moreover, this liturgical aesthetic illuminates the distinctive gift of Black Catholics to the multicultural tapestry of lived faith in the American Church, and might serve as a model for a similar discernment of performative values appropriate to other cultural communities.

This volume complements and expands a body of literature that both explores the contours of African American Catholic practice and situates it within a larger landscape of the life and worship in the Black Church in America. The authors of *Let It Shine!* assume the contextualizing work of Father Cyprian Davis's *The History of Black Catholics in the United States*; Albert Raboteau's *Slave Religion: The*

"Invisible Institution" *in the Antebellum South*; Harold Carter's *The
Prayer Traditions of Black People*; Melva Costen's *African American
Christian Worship*; Eric Lincoln and Lawrence Mamiya's *The Black
Church in the African American Experience*; Diana Hayes and Cyprian
Davis's *Taking Down Our Harps*; Walter Pitts' *The Old Ship of Zion*;
and many others. These authors demonstrate that the renaissance of
Black Catholic worship in the latter decades of the twentieth century,
which is the focus of this volume, is neither an isolated phenomenon
nor a process unique to Roman Catholics. Rather, it is a fitting erup-
tion of the Black religious spirit, cultivated for several centuries in
the Black Church, within the newly "opened window" of Catholic
inculturation. The bibliography that concludes this book offers a
guide to this literature.

The authors of *Let It Shine!* join many others who share an explicit commitment to the continued flourishing of African American
communities and their worship. The goal of this volume is to bring
to light the struggle and dedication that has enabled Black Catholics
to "let their light shine!" and to trim their lamps so that they will
continue to burn brightly into the future. Throughout, the authors
have capitalized "Black" to indicate a critical consciousness—a life-
affirming embrace of Blackness as gift, generative source, and graced
heritage.

LET IT SHINE!

PART ONE   AN HISTORICAL OVERVIEW

The Emergence of African American Catholic Worship

Mary E. McGann, R.S.C.J., and Eva Marie Lumas, S.S.S.

T he religious and social ferment created in the 1960s by Vatican II and the African American Civil Rights movement set the stage for momentous change for Black Catholics in the United States. In the years following these events, the American Church has witnessed the emergence of distinctively African American patterns of celebrating Catholic worship. This chapter will trace the process by which these new expressions of Catholic liturgy have been forged over the past four and a half decades. It will identify the historical forces that served as catalysts; the leadership that has guided the process; the issues, both liturgical and contextual, that have given it direction; the cultural self-redefinition among African American Catholics that has shaped and fostered a reclaiming of a distinct "ethno-religious patrimony" within the larger Church; and the present and future challenges to this process.

Historian Father Cyprian Davis, O.S.B., has brilliantly traced the long history of African American Catholics in the United States.[1] He notes that the earliest baptismal records from St. Augustine, Florida, dating from the second half of the sixteenth century, attest to the presence of Catholics of African descent. Likewise, their presence is evident in Spanish-, French-, and English-speaking territories during the American colonial period.[2] Throughout the ensuing centuries of

3

American history, African Americans were drawn to the Catholic Church for many reasons. Some found within this tradition a sense of stability and order. Others valued Catholic education, which empowered numerous Black children with skills, self-esteem, and moral principles. Still others were drawn by Catholic sacramental practice—the honoring of saints and "holy ancestors," and the rhythms of a liturgical year that appealed to an African cosmology of seasons, times, and creation's impact on worship and daily living.

Yet despite these attractions, the history of Black Catholics in the United States has been marked by frustration and marginalization. Despite their committed engagement in the life of the Church, Black Catholics were systematically excluded from clerical leadership. It was not until 1886 that Augustus Tolton, son of slave parents, became the first recognizable and self-identified Black priest ordained for ministry in the United States.

As early as 1889, African American lay Catholics gave birth to an indigenous tradition of struggle for social justice.[3] Through a series of national Black Catholic lay congresses, held between 1889 and 1924, Catholics of African descent worked "to enjoy the [full] heritage of their faith; to win for themselves, their progeny, and their people, the attention, care and respect of the Church; and to help secure the rights of citizenship for their race."[4]

Black involvement in Catholic liturgical life was likewise marked by both commitment and disappointment. While valuing the sacramental character of Catholic worship, many Black members suffered from liturgies that were dry, uninspired, staid, and lacking in the deep religious feeling that could nourish and express their spiritual longings. In the words of Father Glenn Jean-Marie, "when our people embraced the Catholic faith, they rejected their past in order to become a 'new creation.'. . . [They] left behind Blackness and became pure, White, and Catholic."[5] Brother Cyprian Rowe, S.M. points out that

Catholics of African descent have suffered intensely from the sterility of liturgical rites, because they have somewhere in their bones a tradition of worship in which the sung and spoken word have been fused into celebrations of joy. Afro-Americans are therefore among the first to realize that it is a certain cultural ignorance, and even cultural imperialism, that have resulted in their almost total exclusion from worship, except as spectators.[6]

Two Religious-Liturgical Patrimonies

As faithful and loyal participants in the Catholic tradition, Black Catholics shared another cultural-religious legacy, a tradition well described as "African-American Christianity."[7] This indigenous form of Christian life and worship exceeds the boundaries of any church body, penetrating the fabric of life within the Black community in the United States.[8] African American Christianity was born of Black struggle for liberation, freedom, health, and wholeness in situations of oppression. In pursuing liberation, Black Americans had found "a great Savior, Jesus Christ, the Emancipator."[9] Within the crucible of non-Catholic Christian Churches, African Americans forged a distinctive style of Christian worship, rooted in the expressive patterns of African ritual and expressed through music, preaching, prayer, and testimony.[10] Black Catholics, while participating in Catholic parish life, shared and were nourished by this larger Black religious heritage. Yet this "patrimony" was systematically excluded from their expression of Catholic worship.[11]

The 1960s: A *Kairos* Moment for Black Catholics

The convergence of the American Civil Rights movement and Vatican II in the 1960s set Black Catholics and the entire American Church on a new course. Theologian M. Shawn Copeland identifies the intersection of these two events as a *kairos*[12] moment for African American Catholics. "Change in the social mood without change in the ecclesial mood might have forced Black Catholics in the United States to abandon their centuries-old religious tradition; change in the ecclesial mood without change in the social mood might have compelled them to barter their racial-cultural heritage for silver. There was a propitiousness to these times. This was God's time: this was *kairos*."[13]

On the one hand, the Civil Rights movement challenged the structures of social and economic segregation of Blacks in the United States. It gave birth to a new cultural consciousness, a pride in their God-given worth, that challenged the negative Black identity that had been reinforced in American culture and in the Church itself.[14] It had awakened in Black Catholics a renewed sense of their religious and ritual heritage that had yet to find expression in Catholic life and worship and called into question the persistent racism that denied them full participation and leadership in the Church. In the late 1960s, the first National Black Catholic Clergy Caucus (NBCCC) gathered to address the American bishops on urgent issues that faced the Black community.[15] This initial act of national solidarity among Black clergy was quickly followed by other initiatives to foster Black leadership—clerical, religious, episcopal, and lay.[16] In turn, the new leadership that emerged in the 1960s became highly significant for the unfolding of African American Catholic liturgy.

Within the same decade, the Second Vatican Council challenged the historical cultural, intellectual, and theological insularity of the Catholic Church. The council modeled in an historic way a Church that desires to embrace all cultures, and articulated a vision of a worldwide Church that "respects and fosters the genius and talents of various races and peoples."[17] In embracing a new ecclesial vision, one in which no single culture can be normative for Catholic life and worship, council leaders set a far-reaching course for liturgical inculturation:

> Even in the liturgy the Church has no wish to impose a rigid uniformity . . . rather, the Church respects and fosters the genius

and talents of various races and peoples. The Church . . . preserves intact the elements of these people's way of life . . . and admits such elements into the liturgy itself, provided they are in keeping with the true and authentic spirit of the liturgy. . . . Provisions should be made . . . for *legitimate variations* and adaptations to different groups regions, and peoples. . . . In some places and circumstances . . . an even more *radical adaptation* of the liturgy is needed.[18]

Following the council, two pontiffs gave specific invitations to Catholics in Africa and of African descent to share their religious-cultural heritage with the Church. Pope Paul VI, in his 1969 address in Kampala, invited the churches of Africa to bring "to the Catholic Church the precious and original contribution of 'Blackness' which she particularly needs in this historic hour."[19] His call was taken to refer to Blacks throughout the African diaspora and was often quoted to assert the cause of the Black Catholic movement in the United States. Several years later, John Paul II addressed representatives of the African American Catholic community in New Orleans: "your Black cultural heritage enriches the Church and makes her witness of universality more complete."[20]

Father Clarence R. J. Rivers and the Beginnings of a "Black Renaissance" in Catholic Church Liturgy

Coinciding with the council's welcome of diverse cultural expressions, Father Clarence R. Joseph Rivers was launching what would become a "Black Renaissance" in American Catholic liturgy.[21] Rivers, a musician, dramatist, author, scholar, liturgist, composer, and priest of the diocese of Cincinnati, was convinced that the treasury of African American art, culture, and religious expression could revitalize Catholic worship. Several years before Vatican II, Rivers began composing liturgical music in a Black idiom, producing his *American*

Mass Program in 1963. In his compositions, Rivers drew on the spirituals, jazz, and gospel, thus introducing American Catholics to the rhythms, melodies, and harmonies of the Black musical idiom. Other composers, notably Eddie Bonnemere and Mary Lou Williams, joined Rivers in the attempt to bring the full range of Black music to Catholic worship. However, their use of jazz, calypso, and gospel in liturgical music was not always well accepted and at times openly resisted.[22]

Through workshops and lectures, Rivers worked "to bring greater cultural coherence to the liturgy" by "critically reexamine[ing] the relation of the various elements of the Mass to the Black idiom."[23] In so doing, he began to articulate a specifically African American Catholic liturgical aesthetic, an aesthetic that required (1) the use of drums, highly rhythmic music, musical improvisation, and dance; (2) a ritualized but spontaneous participation of the worshiping community, free of rubrical rigidity; and (3) rich poetic preaching and prayer that draw on participatory drama. This aesthetic is rooted in a theology that knows God to be both transcendent and immanent and flows from a spirituality that acknowledges that "to be spiritual is to be alive, to be capable of moving and of responding to movement."[24] In 1968, Rivers founded Stimuli, Inc.—a center for liturgical arts, design, and publication—to foster a greater synthesis between Black cultural expression and European American worship traditions.[25] He noted that this synthesis would require that Black Catholics come to know and cherish their cultural tradition. Only then could they recognize that its vitality and dynamism can "enrich Christian and other forms of worship not only for Blacks but for all religionists."[26]

The 1970s: Flowering of the Black Catholic Liturgical Movement

The aftermath of the Civil Rights movement left many of the one million Black Catholics in the United States eager for change. The organization of Black Catholic leadership, begun during the 1960s, culminated in the founding of a National Office for Black Catholics (NOBC) in 1970.[27] The same year, the First National Black Lay Congress was held, focusing the lay leadership of Black Catholics on a national level once again. The 1970s saw the naming of four Black bishops in key cities who began to shape an episcopal presence that would take eloquent leadership in the 1980s.[28] Theologians began to formulate a Black Catholic theology, adding their voices to the significant work on Black theology already written by their Protestant brothers and sisters. Historians retraced the historical evolution of Black Catholics, providing first access to the strong if often invisible presence of African Americans in Catholic life in the United States. Together, these leaders precipitated what has aptly been called the "Black Catholic Movement" of the 1970s.[29]

In this context, the American Church saw a flowering of the Black Catholic liturgical movement launched by Father Clarence Rivers in the 1960s. In 1970, Rivers became the first director of the NOBC's Department of Culture and Worship. Through workshops, conferences, and publications, this department began to create a platform for a true indigenization of Black Catholic worship.[30] Under its auspices, the journal *Freeing the Spirit* was launched as a forum for exploring issues pertinent to Black worship, and as a means of providing liturgical resources, images of African art, and newly composed music to pastoral leaders. Black liturgists, composers, and musicians were enlisted to offer workshops on Catholic liturgy around the country. The primary goal of these workshops was to educate and "liberate" Black Catholics to reclaim the fullness of their religious and ritual heritage, and to train ministers for the tasks of leadership. These gatherings enabled composers and musicians to explore various styles of Black sacred music and to collaborate in the creation of new musical settings. Composers Grayson Brown, Robert Ray, Ronald Harbor, and others took up the work of blending the idioms of jazz, gospel, and soul with European musical styles to create a new synthesis: the beginnings of a Black Catholic liturgical repertoire. In the process, Rivers encouraged composers and pastoral musicians to "be free to use traditional 'Catholic' musics and allow them free interplay with our Afro-American musics. . . . Like our forefathers who combined African and white Protestant music to produce the rich musics of Black America, musically liberated Black Catholics . . . [will bring a] still greater enrichment to the Afro-American [musical] styles, [a] further originality."[31]

As leadership articulated the path of liturgical indigenization, Black Catholic renewal began to flourish in pockets around the country. Beginning in the late 1960s, some predominantly Black parishes had taken first initiatives to incorporate African American music, artistic expression, and modes of participation in their worship.[32] "Black Catholics," writes M. Shawn Copeland, "dove into the treasure chest of African American sacred music, lifting up the spirituals, plundering the Baptist hymnal, tracking down organists competent in the Black musical genre and idiom—often from the Baptist congregation across town!"[33] Gospel choirs were formed in several urban parishes around the country. Drums, pianos, and other instruments found a new home in Catholic worship spaces. The first Black lay deacons were trained to add a Black liturgical presence in parishes with white clerical leadership.[34] Liturgical vestments and altar coverings were created in African styles and fabrics. Statuary was replaced with images of African saints. The liberation colors red, black, and green, used by Black Americans in the past and revived during the Civil Rights movement, appeared in Catholic churches. This "reclothing" of church and ministers allowed Black Catholics to say in a new way, "We are here, and we're going to make this Church our home." But not all Black Catholics responded positively to these directions. Resistance due to Catholic training and to a diversity of perspectives signaled a truth that would become clearer in the 1980s: Black culture is not monolithic, but diverse and dynamic.

Black Catholic Liturgical Music

It is not surprising that music was one of the first areas of focus in parish renewal. Black sacred song is perhaps the most comprehensive repository of Black spirituality, theology, cosmology. Spirituals were the first source of African American music to be used by Catholic communities, providing a cultural touchstone that reached back into the roots and early manifestations of Black religious experience in the United States.[35] As Sister Thea Bowman—scholar, musician, poet, and educator—noted:

> African Americans in sacred song preserved the memory of African religious rites and symbols, of a holistic African spirituality, of rhythms and tones and harmonies that communicated their deepest feelings across barriers of region and language. African Americans in fields and quarters, at work, in secret meetings, in slave festivals, in churches, camp meets and revivals, wherever they met or congregated, consoled and strengthened themselves and one another with sacred song—moans, chants, shouts, psalms, hymns, and jubilees, first African songs, then African American songs. In the crucible of separation and suffering, African American sacred song was formed.[36]

The Biblical character of many spirituals made them a desirable expression of Black Catholic worship.[37] Many give voice to a "mystical identification with Jesus, with God, and all the heroes of the Hebrew and Christian scriptures."[38] Spirituals are expressions of faith with strong social implications. Created within a slave environment, they express a longing for radical change, for a freedom and deliverance which the power of God in Jesus can bring about.[39] It is not incidental that during the first decade of Catholic renewal after Vatican II, spirituals were rediscovered as the freedom songs of the twentieth-century Civil Rights movement.[40]

Beginning in the 1970s, the African American gospel music tradition took on new importance for Catholic communities.[41] In assessing this development, ethnomusicologist Jacqueline Dje Dje
points out that gospel music carries a significantly different meaning
than spirituals in Black culture. Spirituals grew out of a rural, South-
ern, slave environment, and thus carry the affective emotions associated with this experience. Gospel music, on the other hand, has its
roots in post–World War I migrations of African Americans, many
of whom were Catholic, from rural settings in the South to urban
centers in the North, and in the changing religious ideas and ideals
that grew from this new sociological environment.[42] Dje Dje proposes that gospel music's reflection of the sensibilities of Blacks in
urban areas gives it a particular attraction for Catholic communities,
since "Catholicism in the United States has essentially been an
urban phenomenon."[43]

Catholic musicians drew on other repertoires of Black sacred
music as well. Hymnody formerly adopted by the Black Church, especially those hymns beloved of African American communities
such as "Blessed Assurance" and "Amazing Grace," were incorporated into Catholic worship. As in Black Church contexts, Catholic
musicians performed these hymns according to Black aesthetic sensitivities, adopting a performance practice that requires improvisation, embellishment, and the dynamic communication of "soul."[44]
In the words of Clarence Rivers, "The essence of Black music is
freedom. When music is free, it is soulful at its source, and soul-
stirring in its effect."[45]

A Black Catholic Liturgical Aesthetic, Theology, and Spirituality

During the 1970s, Clarence Rivers continued his prophetic work of
articulating a Black Catholic liturgical aesthetic. His 1974 *Soulfull
Worship* mined the resources of Black worship for Catholics—the
importance of the spoken word, music, dance, and drama; the centrality of the congregation; and the key role of the pastor. A second

publication, *The Spirit in Worship* (1978), pushed deeper for a true integration of Black culture and Catholic worship. Identifying the African roots of Black worship, Rivers articulated the centrality of "soul" to the Black religious aesthetic. He contended that for worship to satisfy the religious longings of Black Catholics, this quality of "soul" must permeate the entire ritual event—its prayer styles, preaching, and sacramental action. Rivers contrasted the oral/aural, poetic, and holistic predilections of African cultures with the more "ocular," print-oriented, and linear orientations of Western cultures that have shaped the patterns of Catholic worship, demonstrating how the latter mitigates against "soulful" worship.[46]

Liturgical renewal during this period was inseparable from the work of many to retrieve the history of Black Catholics in the United States and to articulate the theology and spirituality implicit in their ethno-religious heritage.[47] In 1977, the NOBC sponsored a national, ecumenical conference on worship and spirituality in the Black community that culminated in the publication of *This Far by Faith: American Black Worship and Its African Roots*. Brother Cyprian Rowe, addressing this symposium, signaled a critical theme: the need to acknowledge the "distinctiveness of Black culture."[48] Rowe stated that the distinctiveness of Black culture is most evident in those "areas of Afro-American life that Euro-Americans were not interested in . . . music and art and church. Those were particular worlds in which [Black] people were not compelled by circumstances to interact constantly with European culture."[49] Likewise, theologian William B. McClain pointed to the centrality of worship in the formation of Black spirituality and theology.[50] The most distinctive element of Black worship, he contended, is its ability to discern and celebrate the presence, power, and victory of God within the pain, struggles, and injustices of Black life. Worship is a central event in the Black community because it symbolizes the inherent worth and worthiness of God's Black creation, and celebrates their God-given power to survive and succeed. Black religious music and song, one of the most distinctive and renowned features of Black ritual, is a rhythmic expression of prayer, enabling people to express their experience of life and death, suffering and sorrow, love and judgment, grace and hope, justice and mercy. But all aspects of Black worship, McClain asserted—the prayers, songs, preaching, movement, gestures, symbolic objects, and the environment—must speak of people's real concerns. Black worship must speak to a people who, in the midst of oppression, pursue liberation, wholeness, and holiness, trusting Jesus, the Emancipator, to be companion and guide.

A third conference participant, Bishop James Lyke, O.F.M., addressed the application of Black cultural considerations to Catholic worship.[51] Lyke maintained that this process must ultimately be carried out on the level of local pastoral ministry, with real people, real congregations, and real life. This requires "a certain inevitable and necessary tension: tension between the charism of leadership and the charism of the people; liturgically, tension between what is given us as guidelines, directives, books, and what the local church discovers in applying them. It is . . . impossible for an official Vatican agency serving hundreds of millions of people all over the world to answer the needs of every cultural and subcultural group. That is what pastoral ministry is for."[52]

Lyke explored the challenges of his own liturgical ministry in the Black Catholic community—the importance of discovering authentic feasts and festivals that celebrate Black experience and the challenge of creating a worship environment that reflects the beauty and history of Black people created in the image of God. He stressed that the vitality of African and African American cultural values honored in the liturgy must overflow to the whole life of the parish and society. "There is no conflict, no contradiction between being Black and being Catholic," Lyke stated. "Quite the contrary. One does a disservice to the Church if one is in the Roman Catholic community and if one is not, at the same time, as Black as one can be."[53]

In 1978, the first Black Catholic Theological Symposium was held in Baltimore. Thirty-three participants addressed a broad range of issues, including Black values and self-concept, an African-based spirituality, and directions for catechetics and pastoral theology, demonstrating in their concerns that a Black Catholic theology is not primarily speculative but holistic and rooted in the experience of a people. In this context, liturgists Fathers Glenn Jean-Marie and Clarence Rivers reiterated that "the whole range of Black culture [must be brought] to bear on our worship efforts."[54] Expressive prayer, vibrant preaching, and spirited singing cannot be isolated insertions but are part of a transformation of the whole symbol system of Catholic worship. Jean-Marie challenged Church authority to allow the composition of new eucharistic prayer texts that "flow from the prayer tradition of Black Folks."[55] Rivers charged Black leaders to develop programs to train Black liturgical ministers, musicians, prayer leaders, and preachers; to educate people to a deeper understanding of worship; and to sustain and challenge parishes where Black culture has already been welcome lest they become "inauthentically Catholic in their scope while becoming authentically Black."[56] He called for increased contact and cultural interchange with the Church in the Caribbean, Latin America, and "Mother Africa." But Rivers also noted a growing ecclesiastical racist backlash that threatened to impede the progress already made. In a bold but truthful statement, Rivers claims that the full recovery of Black spirituality and culture in Catholic liturgy is not only a matter of aesthetics—it is a work of justice. "To consider the problem of Black culture within the Catholic Church as merely or even primarily a question of aesthetic preference is a failure to understand history."[57]

A Black Catholic Rite?

Within the climate of the Black Catholic movement of the 1970s, the first questions were raised about the desirability of a separate liturgical rite, even a separate Church, for Catholics of African descent in the United States. For some, such a separation seemed the only way to avoid a persistent "white bias" in decisions regarding Catholic life and worship. The NOBC had been founded in 1970 to enable the Church "to meet the needs of Black people as a people of dignity," recognizing that their needs are distinct from those of the white Catholic community.[58] A breaking away of Black Catholics was not intended but rather a "'functional separatism' with the ultimate objective of integration" in the larger Church. That same year, A. Donald Bourgeois, professor at Ohio State University, addressing a Black Catholic lay congress "called for a doctrinally orthodox church injected 'with meaning and hope and common life' that would have special relevance for Blacks."[59] The following year, the National Black Catholic Clergy Caucus announced that it would study the potential of an African American rite within the Catholic Church. However, these ideas were opposed as "divisive and harmful" by Auxiliary Bishop Harold Perry of New Orleans, who was then the only Black bishop in the United States, and Emmanuel K. Nsubuga, a Ugandan prelate visiting the United States.[60] The question would resurface in the 1980s, as liturgists and pastoral leaders continued to struggle to find ways by which to release the fullness of Black giftedness within the American Church.

As the 1970s concluded, significant changes were visible in the life and worship of African American Catholics. Yet in spite of many gains, racism persisted within Church life. The American hierarchy had yet to lend major support to the efforts of Black Catholic leaders. At the prompting of the "Call to Action" meeting in Detroit, and with the renewed insistence of Black leadership organizations, the U.S. Catholic Bishops issued their second pastoral letter on racism in 1979, entitled *Brothers and Sisters to Us All*. "Racism is an evil which endures in our society and in our Church," they claimed. But "there must be no turning back along the road of justice, no sighing for bygone times of privilege, no nostalgia for simple solutions from another age."[61]

The 1980s: African American Catholic Liturgy, "Authentically Black and Truly Catholic"

As the 1980s dawned, Black Catholics were poised to claim a new synthesis of their Black and Catholic heritage. But the '80s would also be a time of wrestling with deeper issues of identity, leadership, differentiation, self-determination, and power. All of this had an impact on the development of African American liturgy. In 1984, the Black bishops called upon 1.3 million Black Catholics to share their "precious gifts of Blackness" with the larger American Church. They articulated a direction for liturgical renewal—"authentically Black and truly Catholic."[62] Eight new Black bishops were named during this decade,[63] and Bishop Eugene Marino was made the first Black archbishop in the United States. Working together, these Black bishops become a catalyst within the National Conference of Catholic Bishops for the creation of several national secretariats to address the pressing pastoral and liturgical needs of Black Catholics. In 1987, the first National Black Catholic Congress of the twentieth century met to develop a national pastoral plan for evangelization. This plan gained the approval of the American bishops in 1989. Throughout the 1980s, historians and theologians continued to develop resources for a deeper self-understanding and self-determination on the part of Black Catholics, but this decade would also see the first dramatic split within the Black Catholic community. In 1989, Father George Stallings founded the African American Catholic Community, centered at the Imani Temple in Washington, D.C. His purpose was to "give Black Catholics total control over their faith" and to develop a liturgical rite that reflected their culture and history. His actions raised, and continue to raise, questions about the full implications of the processes of inculturation undertaken by Black Catholics.

What We Have Seen and Heard: Liturgical Agenda for the 1980s

In 1984, ten Black bishops issued their first pastoral letter, *What We Have Seen and Heard* (*WWSH*). The primary focus of the letter is evangelization, a work that must be grounded in the sociocultural and spiritual distinctiveness of the Black community and be effective for all its members. The bishops contended that liturgy is an essential aspect of evangelization—a primary place for Black believers to discover a "homeland" in the Catholic Church. For this to happen, liturgical celebrations must become an "even more intense expression of the spiritual vitality of those who are of African origin."[64] Liturgy in the Black community must be at once "authentically Black and truly Catholic." To be authentically Black, worship must utilize the distinctive Black cultural idiom: in music, preaching, bodily expression, artistic furnishing, vestments, and in the whole tempo of worship. It must release the power of "Black Spirituality," a spiritual heritage rooted in an African past. The bishops identify four major characteristics of Black spirituality: it is at once *contemplative*, sensing "the awe of God's transcendence and the vital intimacy of his closeness"; it is *holistic*, embracing "intellect and emotion, spirit and body, action and contemplation, individual and community, sacred and secular"; it is *joyful*, expressed through "movement and song, rhythm and feeling, color and sensation, exultation and thanksgiving"; and finally, it is *communitarian*, assuming that "the 'I' takes its meaning in the 'we'" and finds its call to holiness within the social body.

The bishops contend that a rich expression of this Black spirituality is possible within the shape of the revised Roman liturgy, with its openness to the "gifts of various races and peoples."[65] For this to happen, however, vibrant preaching and music, the caché of the Black religious heritage, must never "overwhelm the liturgy as a balanced unified action." Rather, word and music should "invite the worshiping community to a more profound participation in the total sacramental experience."[66] Hence, "through the liturgy, Black people will come to realize that the Catholic Church is a homeland for Black believers."[67]

The bishops commend Black liturgists, artists, composers, and musicians who have "tirelessly presented workshops and conferences on Black liturgical expression," and call for continued collaborative work that will release "our rich gifts of Blackness for the whole church."[68]

The State of Black Catholic Liturgy: Bishop James Lyke's Survey

A year before the release of *WWSH*, Bishop James Lyke, one of the bishops who issued the document, conducted a survey of twenty-seven Black leaders in an attempt to assess the state of Black Catholic liturgy in the United States.[69] Based on their pastoral experience, twenty-five respondents to the survey identified indigenous music and dynamic preaching as the "essential elements of liturgical expression for Black communities." They affirmed that lively participation, fellowship, freedom of expression, spontaneity of prayer styles, and animated, indigenous leadership are critical as well. However, when questioned if the "present Roman Rite constrains liturgical expression in the Black community," fifteen of these pastoral leaders answered with a strong "yes," in clear contrast to the conclusions drawn in *WWSH*. The remaining ten felt that the current rite allowed for sufficient balance and freedom. All agreed that spontaneity and emotive expression embody the genius of Black people and are essential to the experience of an "adequately enacted ritual," but some voiced caution lest these dynamic factors "obscure the sense of mystery and symbolism in the liturgy." Thus they signaled an issue that would face Black pastoral leaders well into the future: Which takes precedence, the indigenous sense of Black expressive worship or the currently prescribed structures of Roman Catholic liturgy?

Bishop Lyke offered four observations about the survey's findings. First, he noted that there remains a tension as to whether emotion or intellect, heart or mind will dominate Black Catholic worship.

Second, he acknowledged that despite a common culture and history, Black Catholics are quite diverse, and no single model of liturgy will satisfy all. Third, two key areas of debate remained: how to be "catholic" in the selection of liturgical music, and how to be effective in the employment of preaching styles. Finally, Lyke cautioned that much attention is still needed to the whole "environment" within which Black Catholics worship—the action, the symbols, the liturgical feasts, the heroes and heroines upheld, and perhaps most importantly, the "psychologically oppressive" effect of many church buildings that remain "clothed" in the cultural expressions of other ethnic communities for whom they were built.

Fire in the Pews: A Portrait of Worship and Music in Black Catholic Parishes

In 1987, a documentary on Black Catholic worship entitled *Fire in the Pews* was released.[70] The film focuses on the experience of twelve predominantly Black parishes in eight cities around the country.[71] It includes interviews with parishioners, clergy, and other Black Catholic leaders. The viewer is immediately struck by the abundant display of vital and energized worship; the engaging and powerful styles of preaching; and of richly orchestrated, dynamic and participatory music performed with a sense of "communal passion." The pastor of St. Augustine's in Washington, D.C., attributes this vibrancy to a renewal that flourished in the Black Catholic community in the decade preceding the filming, a renewal signaled by an almost tripling of the membership of St. Augustine's. Members of several of the parishes comment on the importance of their finding a "home" in the Church: a place where they can express their Catholic faith in worship that is free, personal, affective, and full of warmth; that provides "a more outward expression of how the Lord touches us"; that is connected with real-life situations; and that gives people energy for building the Kingdom. They speak of the importance of being able to express their joys, struggles, even weaknesses "because that's where the healing is."

Blacks are attracted to Catholic worship "because of its structure, rubrics, solemnity, pageantry, pomp, and circumstance," comments Father George Stallings, a priest in the archdiocese of Washington, D.C.[72] "We are a theatrical people. . . . Catholic liturgy is drama, it is entertainment, in the holistic sense of entertainment . . . involving the senses, smell, the incense, the eyes, the costumes, the music, the touch, the 'Bread of Life' and the 'Cup of Salvation,' . . . the feel that you get, the embrace." At the same time, Black Catholics bring to Catholic liturgy unique and powerful gifts—among them "our unique ability to break the Word and to savor that Word within the arms of a loving community."[73] In the words of Sister Thea Bowman: "Black people from Africa are people of the Word. Among us the Word is celebrated, it is incarnate, it is embodied in song, in dance, in story, in poetry, in sculpture, in relationships. What you witness in our churches is that embodiment and that celebration of the Word."[74] Stallings goes on to remark that preaching in the Black community is heavily rooted in the Word of God as well as in the experience of Black people. "[Preaching] has to touch the fibre of one's being in order to be effective and in order to bring forth an affective response. . . . If people are going to be fired up to do some-thing for God, they have to feel the power of that Word. The problem in many of our churches is that we have churches that are not on fire with the Word of God. . . . You cannot have fire in the pews if there is ice in the pulpit!"[75]

One of the striking aspects of *Fire in the Pews* is the response, both enacted and verbalized, of many white Catholics who have cho-sen to participate in African American parish life and worship. "The Black Church has gifts the white Church is hungry for," comments Father Michael Phleger, white pastor of St. Sabina's in Chicago. Oth-ers echo these sentiments: "People are looking for more than what is being given. I firmly believe the Black Catholic Community will be the salvation of the Catholic Church in America."[76]

Black Episcopal Leadership and the Creation of National Offices

The national impact of Black episcopal leadership continued to increase during the 1980s. In 1984, Black bishops received approval for a Black Liturgy Subcommittee within the National Conference of Catholic Bishops (NCCB). Two years later the NCCB, in response to the continued call of Black bishops to provide "an effective national structure for the support of Black Catholics"[77] established a Standing Committee for Black Catholics. This was followed in 1988 by the creation of a permanent Secretariat for Black Catholics within the NCCB.[78] The creation of this secretariat was perceived as "a sign of the respect from the hierarchy for the potential of Black Catholics and . . . a particular mark of respect for the Black Catholic bishops who played a major role in obtaining this office."[79]

The Subcommittee on Black Worship, chaired by Bishop Wilton Gregory, working with the Bishops' Committee on the Liturgy, began to address questions of liturgical inculturation and to articulate guidelines for the celebration of the Eucharist. These efforts culminated in the NCCB's publication of *In Spirit and Truth: Black Catholic Reflections on the Order of Mass* (1987).[80] In light of the bishops' liturgical agenda, "authentically Black and truly Catholic," *In Spirit and Truth* focuses primarily on the latter portion of that ideal, "truly Catholic." It begins with the revised "Order of Mass," the "General Instruction on the Roman Missal," and other related documents, assessing how Black Catholics might "utilize fully all the present options [within the revised rite] to bring our cultural treasures to the worship life of the Church we love."[81] Each item of the order of Mass is carefully laid out, with remarks about what options are permitted and comments regarding what might interfere with the flow of the ritual action. Despite the caution that characterizes the document, it concludes with this remarkable statement: "Like all

Catholics, Black Catholics are still experiencing the richness of the renewed liturgy. They have been heartened to witness so many creative and inspiring celebrations of the Church's liturgy. *As they continue to probe the possibilities inherent in the Roman liturgy, they will recognize its limitations as well as its still untapped potential.*"[82] Three years later, the Secretariat for Black Catholics, in conjunction with the NCCB, stated that while *In Spirit and Truth* "provides an excellent model and serves as a worthy signpost," it does not exhaust the requirements of a full inculturation of Black culture in Catholic worship. "African American Catholics are in the process of developing and continuing a tradition," a process that requires serious exploration of "the genuine and authentic African heritage that is ours" and "the powerful gifts of African American culture."[83]

In 1983, the Black Catholic Clergy Conference inaugurated a project to assemble the first Black Catholic hymnal in the United States.[84] Black Catholic composers Rawn Harbor and Leon Roberts, in conjunction with Marjorie Gabriel-Burrow, were invited to collaborate in the study, selection, composition, and arrangement of hymns and service music for the new hymnal. In 1987 *Lead Me, Guide Me* was published. Assessing the impact of the hymnal, M. Shawn Copeland speaks of it as "thoroughly Black and thoroughly Catholic." She concludes that in juxtaposing several traditions—spirituals, gospel, Gregorian plain chant, Black arrangements of "Dr. Watts"–style hymns, as well as Catholic standards and new African American Catholic compositions—the hymnal "recognizes and affirms both the commonality and plurality of Black Catholic experience . . . [and serves as] a sign of some maturity in this long period of indigenization."[85]

Continued Questions Regarding the Full Implications of Liturgical Inculturation

Together with liturgical renewal, education, evangelization, and catechesis were among the strongest focuses of Black Catholic leadership throughout the '80s. Scholars and pastoral leaders Toinette Eugene, Nathan Jones, Sister Eva Marie Lumas, and Bishop James Lyke, to name but a few, developed approaches to evangelization and catechesis that took Black theology and Black experience as starting points and that remained "faithful to both our heritages."[86] Together, they sought to develop a type of catechesis that "offers a liberating experience of religion, faith, and religious education for the whole person, rooted in, attentive and faithful to the common and plural Black Catholic experience." They underscored the truth that revelation for Black persons begins precisely in the Black experience, an awareness that would be articulated as "Africentric" in the 1990s. They recognized that African and African American folklore, music, poetry, and art are carriers of deep religious truth and sensitivity, and that the history, theology, and religious traditions of Black people need to interact with Catholic doctrine in vital and dynamic ways.

This work on evangelization and catechesis posed new questions about the full implications of liturgical inculturation in the Black community and focused discontent with processes of "adaptation" that were still experienced as superficial. How will liturgical prayers have power within the Black community if they do not capture the modes of speaking, the turns of phrase, the aphorisms and proverbs that are bearers of truth in an oral/aural culture? If language, music, dance, and art are carriers of revelation, are they not essential rather than peripheral to the liturgical action? And how can preaching name the action of God in the community if it is not rooted in Black experience, the primary place of God's revelation for the African American Catholic community?

Implications of Ongoing Inculturation:
An African American Liturgical Rite?

Questions regarding the desirability of a separate liturgical rite, even a separate Church, for Catholics of African descent in the United

States that had been dismissed in the 1970s as "divisive and harmful" resurfaced in the late 1980s. During the 1987 National Black Catholic Congress in Washington, D.C., a small group of the delegates attempted to present a proposal for the development of an African American liturgical rite. However, the congress' internal polity kept the topic from being placed on the agenda.[87] Within a month of the national congress, Pope John Paul II spoke to an audience of Black Catholic leaders in New Orleans. The pope reiterated the call for African Americans to present their "gift of Blackness to the Church," but he cautioned the participants, "It is important to realize that there is no black Church, no white Church, no American Church; but there is and must be in the one Church of Jesus Christ, a home for blacks, whites, Americans, every culture and race."[88]

The pope's remarks did not resonate with the ethno-religious self-understanding that characterized the Black Catholic movement of the time. Giles Conwill, a Black Catholic cultural anthropologist, captured the mood of the movement by saying that African American Catholics had begun to speak of their religious specificity as "Black Catholicism" rather than the "Catholicism of Blacks."[89] Conwill described the shift in language as an indication that Black Catholics had moved beyond the Eurocentric confines of the faith they had inherited. They had arrived at "a condition of true indigenization, with Black leadership; a deep, abiding, rooted, and flourishing identity."[90] Nonetheless, their full membership in the Catholic Church remained an elusive goal. In 1989, Sister Thea Bowman addressed the American Catholic bishops:

> Those [of our ancestors] who survived the middle passage [brought] to the American continent . . . treasures of African heritage, African spiritual and cultural gifts [of] wisdom, faith, . . . art and drama, . . . the celebration of life values in an African way and style—in song and instrumentation, in story and drum, in verse and anecdote. . . . Our people . . . helped build this nation,

in cotton and grain, in beans and vegetables, in brick and
mortar. . . . They cleaned houses and built churches, . . . built
railroads and bridges and national monuments. Black people
defended this country, . . . taught and molded and raised
children. . . .

Surviving our history, physically, mentally, emotionally, morally,
spiritually, faithfully, and joyfully, our people developed a culture
that was African and American, that was formed and enriched by
all that we experienced. And despite all this, despite the civil
rights movement in the '60s and the socio-educational gains of
the '70s, Blacks in the 1980s are still struggling . . . *still trying to
find home in the homeland and home in the [Catholic] church.*[91]

The Right to Rites

That same year, moved by the struggle "to find a home in the
church," Father George Stallings founded Imani Temple—a separate
Black but Catholic church of which he later became archbishop. He
argued that for African Americans to fully express their culture and
history in Catholic worship, they needed a specific rite distinct from
the Latin rite of the Roman Catholic Church.[92] Therefore, he adopted
an unofficial English-language version of a liturgical rite approved
by the Vatican for use in the African nation of Zaire.[93] While Stallings' action in creating a separate church was criticized by many
Black Catholics,[94] the question of a more radical adaptation of the
Roman Catholic liturgy was being addressed by Black Catholic leaders. In the summer of 1989, the Joint Conference of Black Catholic
Clergy, Sisters, and Seminarians invited Stallings to explain his actions at their annual convocation. After a lengthy and animated discussion, the conference decided to write Stallings' archbishop in
support of Imani Temple. Two Black bishops offered to be "episcopal
advisors" to the venture.[95] The joint conference proposed that a study
into the need for an African American Catholic rite be placed on the

agenda of the 1992 National Black Catholic Congress.[96] What they envisioned was a canonically autonomous rite, involving both a unique liturgical rite and an autonomous structure of governance.[97] This direction, however, was not embraced by all.

The most ardent opposition to an autonomous African American rite was articulated by Father D. Reginald Whitt, O.P., an African American professor of canon law. Whitt identified several issues that supporters of the rite needed to address.[98] First, he questioned whether the presence of African Americans in the Church was of sufficient duration, and their cultural-spiritual-religious patrimony of sufficient distinction, to warrant status with the twenty-three long-standing canonical rites that constitute the worldwide Catholic community. Second, he queried if autonomy from the Roman rite might relegate Black Catholics to "de facto second class" status and jeopardize their growing influence within the U.S. Episcopacy and the larger Catholic Church. Whitt then asked if the limited financial resources and the relatively small number of priests and pastoral personnel available could adequately serve the more than two million African American Catholics and provide the necessary institutional infrastructure to meet their ministerial needs. Finally, he noted that affiliation with the Roman rite may be the most crucial factor that unifies U.S. Black Catholics and that the formulation of a new rite might jeopardize the needs of Blacks who choose to remain within the Roman Catholic Church. Whitt's passion and scholarship, used here to protest the formulation of an autonomous rite, would reappear in the mid-1990s, revealing a new appreciation of the African American community's ethno-religious patrimony. His energies and expertise would then be directed toward challenging the Church's resistance to formulating new liturgical structures for the African American Catholic community.

Theologian Father Edward Braxton tempered Whitt's somber evaluation while offering an alternative to the autonomous rite initiated by Stallings. He proposed the development of several "authorized liturgical models," paradigms, and examples that could be employed by communities to the extent they wish.[99] To develop these models, Braxton suggested that the American bishops seek approval from the Holy See for an extended period of careful experimentation and creative liturgical development, carried out through the establishment of officially authorized centers for African American Catholic study in strategic places around the country. Here, pastors and scholars could gather examples of unofficial efforts to adapt the Roman rite for Black Catholic communities; establish a network of resource people—poets, musicians, artists, preachers, fabric and vestment designers; determine places where African American Catholic worship had attained a level of excellence; and develop a range of liturgical services to be used on the parish level—Bible services, liturgies of the Word, revivals, devotions to Mary and the saints. In addition, Braxton proposed that several African American Catholics be invited to collaborate with the International Commission on English in the Liturgy (ICEL) in the creation of new eucharistic prayers that use the structure, language, and style of Black worship traditions while remaining faithful to Catholic beliefs. Despite the cogency of Braxton's proposals, no official action was taken.

As the 1980s drew to a close, questions of how to integrate these varied pastoral and liturgical concerns remained a challenge. No matter what their position, most African American Catholics agreed that they had reached a crucial stage as a community. They now stood on the threshold of a new configuration of their faith and faithfulness. Whether or not there was a need for an African American canonical rite was yet to be decided. Only one thing was certain: they would fully participate in making the decision!

The 1990s: The Challenge of Inculturation and the Risk of Separation

Discussion of an African American rite gained momentum in the 1990s. A growing number of African American Catholics now questioned if the full expression of their faith required autonomy from the liturgical, if not the juridical, constraints of a Church that was ignorant of, or at least indifferent to, their specific cultural, spiritual, historical, and sociopolitical realities. In the early 1990s a second episcopal document on African American Catholic worship affirmed the distinct ethno-religious patrimony of the African American community and asserted its rightful place within Roman Catholicism. But the document was criticized by many as too little, too late. They insisted that the liturgical priorities of African American Catholics in the 1990s be guided by the theology of inculturation, the philosophy of Africentricity, and a reiteration of the pastoral need of indigenous leadership. Delegates to the 1992 National Black Catholic Congress affirmed these sentiments, voting for a nationwide opinion survey to assess the desirability of an African American Catholic rite. Although a majority of respondents to the survey rejected the idea of an autonomous canonical rite, they explicitly called for a fuller inclusion of African American culture within their celebration of the Roman rite. Even before the survey results were published in 1995, several significant liturgical innovations had been initiated.

The 1990s witnessed the emergence of new and maturing pastoral leaders: five new African American bishops were appointed; four African American bishops were made ordinaries of a diocese; and one bishop became the vice-chairman (chair-elect) of the National Conference of Catholic Bishops. The number of African American Catholic theologians, scholars, administrators, and authors had tripled since the early 1980s. The 1990s, however, would be marked by a significant loss of leadership within the Black community. Within a single decade, Sister Thea Bowman, Father Bede Abram, Archbishop James Lyke, Brother Joseph Davis, Nathan Jones, Father Glenn Jean-Marie, Bishop Joseph Francis, Bishop Carl Fisher, and Leon Roberts had died, and Brother Cyprian Rowe left the Catholic Church to join

Imani Temple.[100] Through it all, the liturgical insights and the diversity of African American Catholics became more focused. Issues that were raised in the previous three decades resurfaced, but with greater depth, urgency, and conviction.

Plenty Good Room

In 1990, the American bishops, with the Black Liturgy Subcommittee and the Bishops' Committee for Black Catholics, issued a second document, *Plenty Good Room: The Spirit and Truth of African American Catholic Worship*. In contrast to their earlier document, *In Spirit and Truth*, which focused primarily on how African American worship might be "truly Catholic," *Plenty Good Room* placed greater emphasis on the other side of the agenda: "authentically Black." The authors acknowledge that Black culture is not monolithic and that no single approach to liturgical expression will satisfy the religious longings of all African American Catholics. At the same time, they delineate certain dimensions of the culture that have had an impact on Black Catholic worship.[101] African American religious experience, they note, has been shaped by certain African perceptions: the all-pervasiveness of religion, a sense of the holy that encompasses the whole mystery of life, and an understanding of life as a total immersion in a sacred cosmos. These religious sensitivities have been honed within various Christian traditions, as well as the "church of the slave quarters and family gatherings where the spirituals were born, sung, danced, prayed, shouted, sermonized; where the sin-sick soul was healed."[102] The document reiterates that spirituality must be the starting point of a distinctively African American Catholic liturgy. In addition to the four dimensions of that spirituality articulated in *What We Have Seen and Heard*—contemplative, holistic, joyful, and communitarian—the document asserts that African American spirituality has a strongly intuitive and emotive base." For

African Americans, emotion serves as a means of experiencing reality—a way of knowing and learning. "African reason is more *logos* (word) than *ratio* (intellect). For *ratio* is compasses, square and sextant, scale and yardstick, whereas *logos* is living Word, the most specifically human expression of the neuro-sensorial impression. . . . The Black African *logos* in its ascent to the *Verbum* (transcendent) removes the rust from reality to bring out its primordial color, grain, texture, sound and color."[103]

Based on this articulated spirituality, the document highlights certain ritual emphases that mark African American Catholic worship:[104] (1) *space*: like the hush-harbors of the past, a worship space that "gives sway to the rich array of the auditory, tactile, visual, and olfactory senses," communicating both an African heritage and the struggle of Black Americans today; (2) *time*: an unfettered period of time that gives "the Spirit breathing room" and time to "tell the ancient story"; (3) *action*: movements, gestures—"hands lifted in prayer, bowed heads, bended knee, jumping, dancing, shouting"— and bodily interaction that speak of the movements of the Spirit; (4) *the language of prayer and preaching*: vivid narrative, rhythmic intonations, poetry, witnessing, heartfelt calling on God—all signaling that "words are important," and that words become dialogic within the worshiping assembly; and (5) *sacred song*: the "soul" of African American liturgy, full of improvisation, creativity, spontaneity, and response. In conclusion, the authors state that honing authentic African American Catholic worship is a process "of developing and continuing a tradition, and that this "laudatory and difficult task" needs to continue into the future, engaging the "pastoral sensitivity and academic excellence [of] liturgists, scholars, artists, musicians and pastors."[105]

Plenty Good Room was generally embraced by the African American Catholic community as a much-needed affirmation of Black culture, spirituality, and religiosity. However, the limitations of the document could be readily identified. Two severe criticisms of the document were its frequent use of the terms "adaptation" and "accommodation" instead of "inculturation" and its implicit, if not explicit, endorsement of the rubrical prescriptions of the Roman rite as the normative model for Black Catholic worship.[106]

Adaptation or Inculturation

African American Catholics who wanted more self-determinating participation within the Catholic Church pointed to the use of the term "adaptation" in *Plenty Good Room* as further proof of the persistent "white bias" of the American Catholic episcopacy. Criticism of this term in all Roman pastoral directives of the time was likewise being voiced by theologians and pastoral leaders throughout the larger Catholic community. By the end of the 1980s, "adaptation" was no longer understood as a "neutral" term.[107] It was now commonly equated with "cultural accommodation," a process that allows only superficial modifications in the Church's norms and practices and often involves the manipulation of culture to suit established pastoral conventions.[108] A significant number of African American Catholics concluded that the use of this term in *Plenty Good Room* demonstrated the disparity of pastoral vision that existed between the Black community and the U.S. episcopacy. They believed that the growing depth and breadth of the Black Catholic movement required a full embrace of liturgical "inculturation," an ongoing, reciprocal process between faith and culture. This process radically imbues culture with the spirit and values of the gospel such that it is renewed, purified, and more consciously oriented to the ethical norms manifested by the life and teachings of Jesus Christ. At the same time, the faith tradition is embellished by the culture such that it is renewed, further developed, and expanded by the cultural gifts of a particular faith community.

Theologian Ary Roest Crollius gives further definition to the term inculturation by explaining it as a process that includes three distinct and necessary phases. During the first phase, which Crollius calls *translation,* local Church officials (presumably of a different culture than the local community) learn to use the symbols and idiom of the people to promote the faith, and the people learn to articulate their beliefs, traditions, and values within the existing constructs of the faith tradition. Within the second phase, which Crollius names *assimilation,* the faith tradition is no longer a stranger to the people, because there are indigenous pastoral leaders who exercise a primary role in nurturing the local community's faith. As this phase progresses, the local community's articulation and practice of the faith demonstrates increasingly more cultural specificity, which inevitably develops into the third and last phase, *transformation.* At this point, the local faith community's experience of the religious tradition has become an integral part of their self-understanding, and the community's expression of the faith becomes synthesized with the primary symbol systems of its culture.[109] The critics of *Plenty Good Room* believed that the document promoted the second stage, *assimilation,* for a community that had reached the third, *transformational* stage. To support this claim, they readily referred to the Black Catholic bishop's 1984 pastoral letter, which states: "The African-American Catholic community has now come of age. . . . The historical roots of Black America and those of Catholic America are intimately intertwined. Now is the time for us who are Black Americans and Black Catholics to reclaim our roots and to shoulder the responsibilities of being both Black and Catholic. The responsibility is both to our own people and to our own Church."[110]

While the first criticism of *Plenty Good Room* challenged its terminology, the second criticism challenged its goals. The document had been written as a companion to *In Spirit and Truth,* and like its predecessor, *Plenty Good Room* endorsed the Roman rite as the starting point, if not the normative model, for Black Catholic worship.[111] This perception of the document refueled the ongoing discussion of an autonomous African American rite. In 1991, the National Black Catholic Clergy Caucus' African American Catholic Rite Committee

(AACRC) published a monograph entitled *Right Rites*.[112] The document was developed with a fourfold purpose: (1) to explain the nature and origin of Catholic canonical and liturgical rites; (2) to identify the Roman rite (also referred to as the Latin or Western rite) as one of the Catholic Church's twenty-three rites; (3) to identify several of the pastoral concerns of the Black Catholic community; and (4) to propose a study of an African American Catholic rite that would be presented at the 1992 National Black Catholic Congress (NBCC). This proposal read, "We urge the permanent body of the National Black Catholic Congress to initiate, coordinate, and support a comprehensive study to determine the desirability and feasibility of establishing an African American Catholic Rite."[113]

Right Rites urged the establishment of an African American Catholic rite as an essential means of addressing three urgent pastoral concerns: (1) the survival of Black Catholicism; (2) the cultural imperatives for effective Catholic evangelization; and (3) the need for Black Catholic leadership.[114] It maintained that the Catholic Church's failure to embrace fully the ethno-religious patrimony of Blacks was contributing to the demise of the Black Catholic community—forcing Black Catholics to look to other faith traditions and / or ideological foundations to address the pastoral issues that permeated their lives.[115] The NBCCC monograph also charged that the Catholic Church's halfhearted evangelization efforts and Euro-dominant pastoral priorities were primary contributors to the growing "unchurched" population within the Black community, as well as the increasing number of Black Catholics who were supplementing their practice of Catholicism by frequenting other churches.[116] The monograph further maintained that this practice would inevitably continue until the Catholic Church actively pursued full inculturation.[117] Anything less would simply result in perpetuating the dependence of Blacks upon non-Black ecclesial leaders to "interpret the faith for them" and perpetuate the untenable conflicts that arise from Blacks always having to defend and justify their religious insights and sensibilities.

The Study of Opinions

The NBCCC distributed *Right Rites* to the National Black Catholic Congress Office's regional coordinators nationwide with a request that the publication be studied by the delegates to the 1992 National Black Catholic Congress. The proposal was unanimously supported by the congress delegates. In response, the National Black Catholic Congress Office conducted a random survey[118] of the African American community in April, 1994. A report of the survey findings was released in January, 1995, under the title *A Study of the Opinions of African American Catholics.*[119] Seventy-two percent of the respondents rejected the idea of an autonomous canonical rite, but a clear majority (64 percent) said they would welcome the possibility of developing liturgies that were more distinctively Black.[120] A more complete review of the survey data revealed that 79 percent of the respondents felt comfortable in their parish, while 51 percent felt the U.S. Church as a whole did not care about them. Forty-five percent said their parish liturgies already included some form of Black religious expression. However, 50 percent wanted more African American music, 59 percent wanted more African customs incorporated into special religious events (e.g., baptisms and weddings), and 53 percent wanted a distinctive African liturgy developed for African American parishes. Another key indicator in the survey data revealed that almost 55 percent of the respondents believed that predominantly African American parishes should have African American pastors (24 percent disagreed).[121]

The National Black Catholic Congress Office interpreted these findings by issuing a poignant challenge in the concluding statement of the survey report:

> The data shows [*sic*] very little support for, and a great deal of opposition to, the creation of a full canonical rite or for other

opinions or proposals seen as separatist. . . . On the other hand, there is a very strong and even widespread support for an increased African American focus in the church's life and worship, with only the older group offering a little less support. . . . *As a matter of ecclesial strategy, this suggests that the choice is between dealing with Increased African American Focus now or Separation later.*[122]

The report summary goes on to say that local rather than national initiatives to develop liturgies with more of an "African American focus" would be better supported due to the high level of confidence that the survey respondents expressed for their parishes. The National Black Catholic Congress Office further proposed that ecclesial authoritative groups assist these efforts in the following manner: "[B]oth authority groups and professional groups might . . . envision their role as primarily removing roadblocks to local indicatives, sponsoring research and scholarship, providing opportunities for training of clergy, religious and lay leaders, and encouraging parishes which are most successful at implementing a strategy of increased African American focus to share their stories with others."[123]

The survey report concluded with three reflection papers that explored the pastoral and theological implications of the data. The first paper, written by Leonard G. Scott, an African American canon lawyer, concluded that the respondents showed tacit support for the creation of a liturgical rite, like "The Roman Missal for the dioceses of Zaire," if not for an autonomous rite. Scott noted that both the Vatican II *Constitution on the Sacred Liturgy* and the Revised Code of Canon Law acknowledge that such rites may be needed so that people can "follow their own form of spiritual life consonant with the teaching of the Church."[124] Moreover, he concluded that the strong support for more of an "African American focus" in worship demonstrated that Black Catholics do not oppose separatism at the parish level.[125]

A second paper, written by African American theologian Sister Jamie Phelps, O.P., interpreted the survey data as an indication that Black Catholics in the 1990s had embraced two "major theological concepts prevalent within contemporary Catholic ecclesiology: the theology of inculturation and the theology of communion."[126] Phelps interpreted the survey findings as a sign of the African American community's conscious attempt to reclaim their identity as a people and celebrate it with the full rights, privileges, and obligations as other members of the Church. She underscored the fact that inculturation of the Gospels, preaching, and liturgical celebration are essential to the "growth and nurturance of the life and well-being of African American Catholics."[127] She interpreted the rejection of an autonomous rite as a rejection of the "myth of racial inferiority" that once enforced American apartheid in society and the Church. Finally, Phelps proposed that research of this type continue so that the U.S. bishops, as well as other pastoral leaders, might be better equipped to design and implement effective pastoral strategies with / for the African American community.[128]

A third and final interpretation of the survey, offered by African American theologian Diana L. Hayes, posits that several pastoral questions raised in the 1970s and 1980s were now being answered in the 1990s. She summarizes these earlier questions in this way:

How do we, as a people of African roots and American and other branches, come together to sing our songs of faith in a style and manner in which we are comfortable and at home? Must we adapt ourselves to the styles and forms of worship of our Euro-American brothers and sisters who, although they share our faith, do not share our historical experience of enslavement, oppression and continuing discrimination based solely on race, or can we be free to inculturate the Christian faith and its Catholic expression into our own culture and historical traditions showing that they are equally worthy and capable of nurturing and spreading the Gospel. Is there something distinctly "Black" about our expression of "church" which should not only be preserved but also fostered, taught, and passed down to oncoming generations while, at the same time, being shared as an enriching gift with all whom we come into contact![129]

According to Hayes, the survey data showed the awareness and resolve of a community that is decidedly Black and Catholic. African American Catholics were no longer asking for acceptance; they were asking for recognition and understanding. But, more than this, they were asking for reconciliation and healing in a Church marred by racism; and, if this was to happen, the larger Church and the Black community must interact as equals.[130] Hayes concluded by saying that African American liturgical innovations bear witness to their "coming of age" in ways that are "neither transient nor precipitate." Such innovations express the community's efforts for a fuller experience and expression of their faith tradition. In the last analysis, she concludes, "there is no turning back."[131]

With the survey completed, NBCCC's committee for an African American rite disbanded. Some African Americans questioned if the respondents would have given more support to an autonomous rite had they understood that it would be "in communion with Rome" while maintaining its own structures of governance. Others questioned how much the hurtful legacy of American apartheid, as well as the 1990s pastoral emphasis on "multiculturalism," had influenced the respondents' rejection of what seemed to be a separatist movement. Some questioned whether or not the respondents understood the significant role that their historic "separate Church" experience had played in helping them both to name and develop their distinct ethno-religious identity.[132] Still others believed that the issue of an African American Catholic rite had been resolutely decided. However, the confluence of several developments within the larger

Black community and the African American Catholic community during the early 1990s served to keep the discussion very much alive.

Africentricity as a Means of Inculturation

One of the most important developments of the early 1990s was the growing popularity of "Africentricity"[133] as the galvanizing principle or philosophy within the African American community. African American Catholics were not unaffected by its insight or appeal. The African American scholar Molefi Asante had popularized the term "Africentricity" in 1980 to describe the activity of Black people around the world who were consciously reclaiming an African world-view, as well as the cosmic or metaphysical realm that determined what it meant for them to be human persons. By 1991 Asante had further developed the concept. He argued that his word, more than any other image (e.g., a Black interpretation, and African American perspective), denoted the deliberate effort of Black people to name themselves, value themselves, pursue their legitimate ambitions, and promote their insights from a self-conscious and self-accepting frame of reference. Moreover, Asante maintained that this philosophical stance did not seek to denigrate the inherent merits or worth of any other cultural heritage. It simply asserted that African culture represents an alternative vision to the worldview, epistemology, cosmology, normative assumptions, and axiological frames of reference that have dominated human discourse, human relationships, and human industry for the last five hundred years.[134]

While the ideational constructs of Africentricity are clearly evident in the theological and pastoral literature written by African American pastoral leaders throughout the 1970s and 1980s,[135] the term was formally introduced into Catholic pastoral literature in relationship to catechesis in 1995.[136] By that time the NCCB Subcommittee on Liturgy in the African American Community had been disbanded. In the absence of an episcopal committee sensitive to the liturgical needs and priorities of African Americans, the pastoral leadership of the Black Catholic community was left on its own to develop the community's liturgical life in more culturally relevant ways. As the decade progressed, pastoral leaders in various parts of the country created a rich constellation of liturgical innovations. The following list highlights only a sampling of noteworthy examples. The National Black Catholic Congress Office published *Rise Up and Rebuild,* a ritually based catechetical process that blends traditional Catholic prayer forms (e.g., antiphonal prayers) with characteristic elements of the African American prayer tradition (e.g., music, aphorisms, and aesthetics) and ritual actions that originated in traditional African worship (e.g., the pouring of a libation to the ancestors).[137] Sacramental celebrations were enriched as a growing number of Black pastoral leaders incorporated elements of African naming ceremonies into the celebration of baptism and created rites of passage as a distinctive mode of preparing Black youth for confirmation. Black leaders collaborated with the North American Forum on the Catecheumenate to consider Africentric strategies for the Order of Christian Initiation for Adults. A nationally representative group of Black liturgical composers and musicians began to work on a book of Black psalmody.[138] A cooperative of Black diocesan and parish pastoral leaders proposed ways to utilize African proverbs to explicate the Sunday gospel readings. A culturally distinct genre of liturgical prayers, blessings, and commissioning rites for parish ministers began to develop. Catholic liturgical celebrations of Black History Month became commonplace nationwide. The NBCCC designated November as Black Catholic History Month and encouraged the development of parish liturgical celebrations. The introductory rite of parish eucharistic celebrations sometimes included an invocation of the ancestors. Black pastoral leaders had begun to explore the ethnoreligious significance of the liturgical year. The celebration of Kwanzaa began to influence the way African American Catholics celebrated Christmastide.[139] Liturgical dance became a more frequent occurrence in African American Catholic worship. Culturally specific ritual texts for the celebration of traditional Catholic devotions (e.g., Marian feasts) began to emerge.

Another significant development in the 1990s was the creation of an African American Catholic liturgical journal, *Plenty Good Room*, with its inaugural issue appearing in June, 1993. The purpose of the publication, as described by editor Father J-Glenn Murray, S.J., was to aid Catholic liturgical ministers who "strive for union of rite and culture" in the African American Catholic community. The journal met with mixed reviews from the African American community.[140] Its feature articles were generally lauded for the "continuing education" they provided for parish liturgical ministers and the ongoing catechesis they offered to the larger parish community. However, the theological hermeneutic that undergirded the journal's "practical liturgical suggestions" was often criticized for being "too closely allied" with the rubrical boundaries, and therefore the Eurocentric biases, of the Roman rite. At the same time, this journal provided the only public forum in which the issues of African American liturgical inculturation could be regularly addressed.

Varietates Legitimae

Within this pastoral and liturgical milieu, the Vatican's Congregation for Divine Worship and the Discipline of the Sacraments (CDWDS) issued its 1994 pastoral instruction, *Inculturation and the Roman Liturgy (Varietates legitimae)*—a document that would spark heated debate within the Black Catholic community. The purpose of *Varietates legitimae* was to further clarify the intent of Articles 37–40 of the constitution *Sacrosanctum Concilium,* which addressed the "adaptation of the liturgy to the temperament and conditions of different peoples."[141] The document affirms that liturgical "inculturation" rather than "adaptation" is the normative approach for achieving its objectives. It calls for ongoing research and discernment regarding inculturation in response to each cultural community's "progressive maturation in faith" and highlights the ways in which this was done in the early Church as Christianity spread beyond the boundaries of Jewish religiocultural communities.[142]

The last three sections of *Varietates legitimae* outlined the theological, pastoral, and canonical considerations that should guide all Roman Catholic liturgical inculturation and established a series of foundational principles that should guide the process. Moreover, they identified the document's underlying objectives: (1) to promote the cultural adaptations *already* approved for use in the celebration of the Roman rite, and (2) to preserve "the substantial unity of the Roman rite." Regarding the first, *Varietates legitimae* encouraged the continued liturgical use of a people's language, religious tradition, gestures and postures of prayer, and religious aesthetics (i.e., visual art, architecture, vestiture, the selection and arrangement of decorations, the location of the altar, and the place from which the Scripture is proclaimed).[143]

With regard to the second, preserving the unity of the Roman rite, *Varietates legitimae* articulated five explicit directives. First, it named the national conferences of bishops as the authorized agents who would discern and oversee the manner in which any liturgical adaptations would be implemented, while reserving ultimate authority for determining the merits of these endeavors for the Holy See.[144] Second, it identified criteria for the planning and implementation of liturgical inculturation, instructing the bishops to be mindful of three essential factors: the goal of inculturation, the substantial unity of the Roman rite, and the role of competent authority.[145] Inculturation, the document reiterates, "responds to the needs of a particular culture and leads to adaptations which still remain part of the Roman rite," enabling each cultural community to "fully and actively" participate in the rites while preserving the character of their traditional structures and expressions.[146]

A third directive focused on the need for prudence, reminding the bishops that any and all adaptations of the liturgy should "grow organically from forms already existing" within the Roman liturgical rites.[147] Hence, adaptations that foster religious syncretism, or cause a community to become inward-looking or to use inculturation for political purposes, or that promote an extreme cultural localization of liturgical celebrations, are to be avoided, since these might diminish "the truth of the Christian rite and the expression of the Christian faith."[148] Rather, all adaptations must preserve the liturgy's ability to be "a sign and instrument of unity [within] the Roman rite."[149] A fourth directive reiterated the need for revisions of the liturgical books so as to insure that the Roman missal "remain a sign and instrument of unity," and underscored that only the approved texts, gestures, and order of service are to be used.[150] The final directive addressed those instances when more "radical adaptations" of the rites are deemed necessary. Even in these cases, the document asserts, such changes will occur within the current context of the Roman rite, rather than necessitating a comprehensive transformation of the Church's liturgical rites.[151]

Within months of its publication, *Varietates legitimae* had spawned a furor of debate among African American Catholics. Most agreed that the document simply underscored the insights already articulated by *In Spirit and Truth* (1988) and *Plenty Good Room* (1990). Yet many criticized it for failing to acknowledge the plethora of liturgical insights and innovations that had developed in the decades since Vatican II. For them, *Varietates legitimae* was further proof of the Catholic Church's ignorance, if not distrust, of culture and a contradiction, or at least a misrepresentation, of the pastoral insights of *Sacrosanctum Concilium* and other conciliar and postconciliar documents.

More Than a Question of Starting Points

Critiquing the strengths and weaknesses of *Varietates legitimae* became the focus of a series of feature articles published in the liturgy journal *Plenty Good Room*. In a first essay, then Marist Brother Cyprian Lamar Rowe ardently objected to the notion that "preserving the

unity of the Roman rite" should be a guiding principle for inculturation because it placed predetermined limits on the process. Rowe
maintained that compliance to *Varietates legitimae* would make African Americans little more than "cultural hostages," whose freedom
to engage their ethno-religious identity with Catholicism at the most
personal and compelling level would be diminished, if not disal-
lowed.[152] Simply put, Rowe charged that African Americans should
not accede to the Vatican document's directives without asking the
question, "What gets lost?"

Father J-Glenn Murray, the journal's editor, responded to Rowe
by conceding that *Varietates legitimae* did not offer the most insightful definition of inculturation, but since it was the only one "offered
for the whole church's consideration," he chose to focus on the document's positive aspects.[153] He contended that the document's purpose was to affirm the relationship between faith and culture, and to
introduce the concept of inculturation, rather than adaptation, as the
normative mode for exploring this relationship. Moreover, he
claimed, the definition of inculturation given was "serviceable" because it invited African Americans to create a place for themselves
within the Roman rite.

In a second article, Rowe criticized Murray's position on the
grounds that it did not reflect a plethora of African American philosophical, theological, or pastoral insights.[154] He challenged Murray
to attend to the deeper issues—to critique the insular cultural imperialism of *Varietates legitimae* that minimized the best of the Catholic
Christian tradition, as well as the ethno-religious legacy of the African American community. Rowe proposed that the gravity of the
matter required an ongoing dialogue between the Holy See, the National Conference of Catholic Bishops, and a significant number of
African American Catholics.

Murray responded to Rowe's second article by reviewing the
many ways that the revised liturgical books already invited and embraced African American ethno-religiosity. He identified explicit parallels between the primary symbols of the Black struggle for

liberation and the Christian hunger of salvation.[155] Murray then argued that part of the current emptiness that many African American Catholics experience in their worship is not the fault of the ritual, but rather a lack of cultural and liturgical insight on the part of those persons who prepare and participate in it.

Murray then invited Richard McCarron, a Euro-American doctoral student and friend, into the dialogue. Summarizing the debate thus far between Rowe and Murray, McCarron maintained that they had arrived at divergent conclusions regarding the merits of *Varietates legitimae* because their respective critiques had begun at different starting points.[156] Murray's position was rooted in the liturgical rubrics of the Roman rite; Rowe's was rooted in the distinctive ethnoreligious patrimony of the African American community. McCarron further suggested that their conflicting understandings of liturgy revealed divergent ecclesiologies that should be named and explored. He then challenged both authors with a series of questions. He queried if Murray's defense of the Roman rite underestimated both the Eurocentric biases that undergird current liturgical norms and the spiritual quests of the African American Catholic community. He likewise questioned if Rowe's insistence on an African American rite unduly discredited the potential of the Roman rite to promote the spiritual sojourn of African Americans, while at the same time minimizing the risks of insularity within the Black Catholic community.

Before leaving the Roman Catholic Church to become a bishop of Imani Temple, Cyprian Rowe submitted a rebuttal to McCarron.[157] Rowe not only denounced the Church's cultural imperialism but also criticized the cultural insight of both McCarron and Murray. He expressed concern that Murray's admitted ignorance of significant Black philosophers, theologians, scholars, and cultural theorists impeded his ability to interpret *Varietates legitimae* meaningfully for the African American community. Admitting that McCarron's questions had provoked appropriate self-reflection, he noted that they might have been more helpful if they had come from someone more knowledgeable of, and engaged with, Black culture and religiosity. Rowe restated that the critical flaw of *Varietates legitimae* was its attempt to anticipate the outcome of the inculturation process before it had begun. The real problem, he argued, is one's starting point: if the Roman hierarchy, or anyone else, begins a dialogue about liturgical inculturation without the assumption that both the liturgy *and* the discussants will be changed, there is no real dialogue. Nor can there be any true inculturation. Inculturation will only succeed, he contended, if all participants engage with each other as peers, as "servants of one another."

Both McCarron and Murray responded to Rowe.[158] McCarron restated his intent to "raise issues and spark an ongoing dialogue." Murray repeated his support for the inculturation process that had begun and acknowledged that liturgical inculturation in the African American community could be greatly enhanced if it were better informed by the prophetic insights of more Black pastoral leaders. Moreover, Murray invited Black scholar Father Joseph A. Brown, S.J., to enter the dialogue. Brown's essay attempted to mediate what had become a highly emotional and personal debate.[159] He affirmed Murray's credentials as a liturgist and as a Black Catholic leader. He proposed that Rowe's remarks did not represent the larger African American Catholic community so much as Rowe's own internal struggle while choosing to join Imani Temple. Yet Brown never really addressed Rowe's primary question: *What gets lost? What does the Church as a whole, and African Americans in particular, have to give up in order to accommodate the traditional liturgical structures and expressions of the Roman rite?*

A final article, volunteered by Scott Haldeman, went more to the heart of the matter.[160] He proposed that Murray and Rowe were arguing from a faulty essentialism. He affirmed that some African Americans are at home within the Roman rite, while others require more than the current norms can offer. Both groups, he contended, should have the freedom to satisfy their spiritual longings. Yet the question of what gets lost must be addressed. African Americans may choose to leave behind or suppress certain elements of their culture in order to embrace fully the rubrical norms of the Roman rite. But, he queried, are they choosing to leave these elements behind, or are they being forced to do so?

No Turning Back

Ironically, the most emphatic criticism of *Varietates legitimae* was voiced by Father D. Reginald Whitt, an African American professor of canon law at the University of Notre Dame, who just five years earlier had argued against the creation of an African American rite.[161] While conceding that the document's strength lies in its tacit support for the insights of the Catholic bishops' earlier statements on Black Catholic worship, Whitt offers a comprehensive critique of *Varietates legitimae*'s weaknesses. First, he criticizes the document's claim that *Sacrosanctum Concilium* (*SC*) did not envision that inculturation efforts would transform the Roman liturgical heritage. Rather, he contends, the Vatican II document says nothing about maintaining "the substantial unity of the Roman rite" when discerning the need for a profound inculturation of the liturgy. Moreover, *SC* [no. 40] explicitly acknowledges that certain ethnocultural contexts might *require* the transformation of the Roman rite and/or the creation of new ritual structures. Whitt cites four relatively recent initiatives, approved by the Vatican, that reflect definitive departures from the Roman ritual context: the restoration of the Ambrosian (1974) and the Hispano-Mozarabic (1988) liturgical rites; the creation of a Zairean liturgical rite (1988),[162] which Whitt contends "may constitute a phenomenon just short of a new Latin ritual heritage";[163] and finally, the Church's permitting "at least five Latin Catholic congregations of former Episcopalians in the United States to use the *Book of Divine Worship*, a slightly modified version of the 1979 American *Book of Common Prayer*," for their celebrations of the Eucharist, morning and evening prayer, baptisms, and funerals. The purpose of the latter was to allow them "to keep as much of their 'Anglican heritage' as possible."[164]

Whitt's second critique is that the *Varietates legitimae* offers no guidance for liturgical inculturation within those ethnocultural communities "whose religious culture is Christian but has not customarily been expressed within the Roman liturgy," citing African American religious culture as a primary example.[165] He warns that restricting the inculturation process of African American Catholics to the rubrical confines of the Roman rite may result in the manipulation of African American Christianity—an essentially non-Catholic Western faith tradition with its own "cultural and historical axis." Moreover, he posits that the ongoing efforts of Black Catholics to develop their distinctive ethno-religious heritage may lead to the formulation of inculturated theologies that would require the creation of African American Catholic liturgical rites.

In a third critique, Whitt posited that *Varietates legitimae's* selective reference to the pastoral insights of *Sacrosanctum Concilium* and other counciliar and postconciliar documents contributes little to a renewed understanding of Catholic liturgy; nor does it elucidate the relationship between liturgy and the cultural context that constitutes a people's ethno-religious patrimony.[166] Indeed, the theological and pastoral cautions set forth in the document ignore the need to revise Roman liturgical books continuously in light of the unfolding dynamics of cultural growth and change. These ritual revisions, which in the case of Black Catholics might be extensive, could in turn provide conclusive evidence of the need for an African American Catholic canonical rite. Finally, Whitt recalls that nearly two-thirds of the respondents to the NBCC's 1993 opinion survey supported an increased African American cultural emphasis in the liturgy, and urged African American pastoral leaders to continue their inculturation efforts, even when these endeavors entail more "profound adaptations" of the Roman rite. He encouraged the National Conference of Catholic Bishops to reexamine the ongoing impact and effectiveness of *In Spirit and Truth* as well as *Plenty Good Room*. In sum, Whitt concluded that rather than "cast doubt on its salience, *Varietates legitimae* has breathed additional vigor into the issue of an 'African American Catholic rite.'"

Whitt's 1997 article demonstrated a marked departure from his earlier stance in *Not Rite Now!* The first article questioned whether African American Catholics had a distinct spiritual and religious tradition, and suggested that participation in the Roman rite might actually be *the* primary influence in shaping their ethno-religious identity. His later article revealed a growing awareness that even though the spiritual and religious traditions of Black Catholics had been suppressed within the Roman Church, they were not destroyed.[167] African American Catholics had not simply "discovered" Blackness during the Civil Rights movement; rather, they had begun to explore its legacy in more deliberate ways.[168] For Whitt and a sizable majority of other African American Catholics, the time had come for the pastoral imperatives of both Blackness and Catholicism to work together. Some Black Catholics might decide that full inculturation requires autonomy from the Church of Rome. Others might decide that inculturation can be achieved within the Roman ecclesial structure. In either case, African American Catholics will have the benefit of being intentionally, rather than habitually, Catholic.

Conclusion

> We will go, we shall go, we must go,
> to see what the end can be.[169]

As the third millennium of Christianity begins, it is clear that the forging of a truly African American expression of Catholic liturgy has been, and continues to be, a complex, challenging, and dynamic endeavor. Over the past four decades, African American Catholics

have engaged in a cultural renaissance that has led them to reclaim
their distinct "ethno-religious patrimony" within the larger Church.
At the same time, their spiritual renascence has led to a forthright
assertion that their embrace of Catholicism need not—indeed must
not—require the diminishment of their Blackness. Many issues,
both liturgical and contextual, continue to be debated. New initiatives
and leadership continue to emerge, and each gives witness to new
expressions of joy and pain. Some are satisfied with the liturgical
parameters of the Roman rite. Others are confident that the Church
is open to the ongoing development of more culturally explicit worship within the African American community. Still others are convinced that Roman Catholic liturgical priorities and directives show
more suspicion than support for the spiritual inheritance and quests
of African Americans. Will this divergence of views encourage ongoing renewal within the Roman rite? Yes. Will it contribute to the
Church's ongoing exploration of the relationship between faith and
culture? Yes. Will it occasion the creation of African American liturgical rites? One has only to review the grassroots liturgical innovations of the past four decades to know that the answer to this
question is also "Yes!" Only two questions remain unanswered:
What role will the institutional leaders of the Catholic Church choose
to play in each of these endeavors? And what pastoral priorities will
determine the role they choose?

If the Roman magisterium has definitively decided that the post–
Vatican II "time of experimentation is over," they can only succeed
in forcing African Americans into antagonistic relationships with the
Roman rite. If they are receptive to inculturation as an open-ended
process, however, they can facilitate the spiritual maturity of the
Black Catholic community in ways that will surely ennoble and enrich the whole Church. This understanding of inculturation will require the Church to actively encourage and support the theological
inquiries, pastoral training opportunities, ritual experimentation,
and ongoing dialogue advocated by Vatican II and most postconciliar

liturgical directives. It will require an acknowledgment that Black Catholics must assume the leadership for directing these efforts. It will also require a commitment to forthrightly address the unavoidable tensions and ambiguities of charting a course into an unknown future. Ultimately, it will require that everyone engaged in the enterprise presumes the unfailing providence of God, the pertinence of each person's contribution, and the inherent worth of an ethnoreligious patrimony that is "authentically Black and truly Catholic."

PART TWO   THE FOUNDATIONAL VISION

Clarence R. J. Rivers' Vision of Effective African American Worship

Mary E. McGann, R.S.C.J.

W ithin the social ferment and religious redefinition of African American Catholic life and worship that we have just explored, one figure stands out: that of Father Clarence R. J. Rivers. Best known as a musician and composer, Rivers was likewise a liturgist, poet, dramatist, scholar, and priest of the diocese of Cincinnati whose charismatic leadership fueled the renaissance of Black Catholic worship during the 1970s and 1980s. Having introduced Rivers' work in Part One of this volume, this chapter probes more deeply into his vision of a revitalized and effective worship for African American Catholics and asks what salience it might have for the contemporary Church.

Rivers' vision, articulated during the 1970s,[1] can be summed up in a single insight: for Black Catholics to reclaim their rightful heritage, the whole of Catholic liturgy must be suffused with the religious intuitions and artistic predilections of African American religious culture.[2] Implicitly, he recognized the grace and the challenge of hybridity[3]—the richness of a Catholic worship practice transfused with the wellsprings of Black American culture; a fusion of horizons at once African, American, Black, and Catholic. He believed that the cultural-religious insights of Black Christianity could unlock the potential of Catholic worship not only for Black Catholics,

but for many in the American Church who yearned for deeper renewal. Writing when the word "inculturation" had barely been
coined,[4] Rivers understood its urgency, and recognized that any true
inculturation will be an interculturation—an interpenetration of traditions, a mutual gift exchange in which both Catholic worship and
African American religious culture will be changed and enriched.[5]

Rivers' vision was shaped by several forces. First, his knowledge
and love for Catholic worship, fostered by his priestly formation and
ritual leadership, were enhanced by his study of liturgy, including
doctoral studies at the Institut Catholique in Paris.[6] Second, his gifts
for musical composition, as well as his love of drama and English
literature, cultivated through graduate studies at Xavier, Yale, and the
Catholic University of America, strongly influenced the performative
sensibilities he brought to Catholic worship. Third, his immersion
in African American culture, his love and esteem for its beauty, enabled him to sense its potential gift to Catholic practice. Although a
cradle Catholic, he was familiar with the worship of the traditional
Black Churches and had worked with other Black ministers to discover the meeting points between the prayer styles of the Black
Church and the traditional patterns of Catholic liturgy.[7] Finally, he
was an Africanist in his own right, having spent an extended period
of time in Ghana searching out the roots of Black religious ritual and
the arts. His books and the journal he edited, *Freeing the Spirit,* are
filled with images of African art and sculpture, dance and musical
performance, which evoke in the reader the pulsing rhythms of African improvisatory music and the densely interactive patterns of African ritual and dance.

Rivers' first major publication, *Soulfull Worship* (1974), mined the
resources of Black worship for Catholics—the importance of the spoken word, music, dance, and drama; the centrality of the congregation; and the key role of the pastor. His second, *The Spirit in Worship*
(1978), pushed deeper for a true integration and interpenetration of

Black religious culture and Catholic worship. Both volumes comprise essays, lectures, sermons, newly composed prayers, and liturgical resources. Yet a close reading of the text reveals a cogent and comprehensive approach to the revitalization of Catholic worship specifically for African American communities.

At heart, Rivers' concern was not simply that worship be more culturally resonant, religiously appropriate, or expressedly African American in style, but that worship become truly *effective* for Black Catholic communities.[8] For Rivers, *effective worship* has several recognizable characteristics. First, it nourishes the human need for transcendence—that is, it lifts people up, draws them beyond the here and now, quenches their thirst for God, opens them to God's Word, enables them to praise God for God's goodness, and grounds them in the witness of Jesus Christ that, despite the fragility and frustrations of life, there is a living God who knows their struggle and is ultimately trustworthy. Second, effective worship addresses the real needs and concerns of those who participate. Psychologically, Rivers notes, this means that the worship is rooted concretely in the human life it attempts to symbolize, while strengthening and deepening it. Theologically, this means that it meets the biblical criteria reiterated by all the Hebrew prophets: that worship truly pleasing to God cannot be divorced from an active concern for the needs of the human community. A third characteristic, one that challenges the assumptions of many who practice Catholic liturgy, is that for worship to be effective, it must be enjoyable—open to the joy that dilates the heart, puts mind and body at ease, and draws the spirit into the delight of God's ever-abiding nearness. "If people return to worship as they do to the dining table," stated Rivers, "with eager anticipation of having their hungers satisfied, they have been graced with the gift of effective worship."[9] The very sacramentality of Christian worship, he claims, rooted in the incarnation of Jesus, demands such enjoyment. Finally and most importantly, effective worship leads to *metanoia*—that ongoing conversion of heart and renewal of spirit that changes people's perspective and shapes them into disciples who participate fully in Jesus' mission in the world to be messengers of Good News, caring for the poor, freeing the oppressed, and bringing God's kingdom to birth in the world.

Cultural-Religious Foundations for a Performative View of Effective Worship

With his goal clear, Rivers identified several religious-cultural predilections that he believed were foundational for effective worship in African American communities. Each touches on the enactment of liturgy, while at the same time revealing implicit theological roots. We will explore each of these in some detail before moving to Rivers' performative question: how do they become integral to the practice of worship?

The Dynamic Presence of the Spirit of God—A Biblical Pneumatology

In African American Christianity, and especially in Black Church worship,[10] the active presence of the Holy Spirit is consciously engaged—waited upon, expected, and welcomed. This intuition of the presence of God's Spirit, Rivers claims, is profoundly biblical.[11] Yet, he points out, the roots of this pneumatological perspective reach back beyond the arrival of enslaved Africans on American soil, beyond their encounter with Christianity and therefore with the biblical narratives. In traditional African religion, "the heritage of our foreparents, the main thrust of religious practices is to achieve harmony with the spirits [of the High God] and empowerment by the spirits."[12] This cultural orientation, he notes, prepared Black communities to recognize in the Bible a God who brings life, energy, and power through God's Spirit—who

> breathed that Spirit into motionless clay and made it a moving, living soul; a God [whose] Spirit could turn a stagnant sprawl of

lifeless bones into a moving dance of life; a God [whose] Spirit could stir the waters and make the waters capable of sustaining and renewing life; a God [whose] Spirit could move [persons] to dream divine dreams and speak in the name of God; a God who could break down the barriers of speech that separate people; an unconventional God that disregarded ordinary standards of propriety, by whose Spirit one was commissioned to prophesy, even in the name of and for the benefit of the poor and the dispossessed.[13]

From a Christian perspective, this Spirit of God—a living breath, the *ruach* of God—is divinity poured out and manifest in Jesus' life-giving mission, and imparted to all believers in the pentecostal outpouring of their baptism.

Rivers contends that in traditional African American worship, communities sense that the Spirit of God is present and active when their worship and its music are intensely expressive and moving—when people experience that spiritual power has been released and a new way has been opened before them. What Rivers identifies here is an "effective pneumatology," operative in traditional Black worship, that expects the Spirit to be active in worship, to change and reorient people to the reign of God.[14] From this perspective, worship that does not touch, strengthen, and transform people's lives is simply a poor vessel for the Spirit's action.

Belief in the potency of the Spirit's action, Rivers proposes, is the basis of a "theology of soul"[15] that resides deep in African American culture. As a potent philosophical and theological term in the Black Church, "soul," he points out, is deeply embedded in both African and biblical perceptions of the spiritual and of spirituality. From this perspective, worship is spiritual, is of God's Spirit, when it is "soulful." "Soul," moreover, is a primary aesthetic criterion for how persons participate in Black worship. To sing, preach, or pray "with soul" is to do so from the very depths of one's being, from the "core of one's aliveness." Soulful performance moves and in-spires, in the root sense of that word, because its aliveness and intensity are a manifestation of the power of the divine Spirit, the source of human soul. To participate soulfully in any aspect of worship is to become an instrument of the Spirit, a vessel of divine power moving within the assembly. It is to give witness to one's faith—not in precepts or concepts, but by revealing the embodied presence of God within oneself. Ultimately, it is the community as a whole that discerns and confirms that God's Spirit is truly at work in the soulful expression of an individual, signaling through their words and gestures that power has been released—that "the Spirit was here today!"

While powerfully evident in Black Church worship, Rivers reminds us that "soul" is the biblical legacy of all Christians and the natural heritage of all people. He recalls the words of Jesus to the Samaritan woman, "God is spirit; and those who worship God must worship in Spirit and truth" (Jn 4:24). Soulful worship, realized in African American communities, is thus eminently Catholic and can release a new depth of awareness of the Spirit's vital presence.

Creation as Inherently Good—A Sacramental Worldview

An African worldview, Rivers points out, is inherently sacramental[16]—that is, it assumes that human persons and all of the created world are inherently good.[17] From this African perspective, God's animating spirit, God's àshe, is the life force, the spiritual power that surges through the universe, animating creation and residing in human persons.[18] Hence, God delights in all of God's creation, just as it is. The very qualities that mark God's created universe—movement, color, sound, and the "livingness" of all creatures—delight the One who makes and sustains life, as they are refracted in the rhythms and vibrant responsiveness of a worshiping community.

Within this African worldview, the sacred and the secular are not two spheres of human existence, but deeply penetrate each other. This nondichotomous way of understanding and living in the world,

Rivers notes, is richly resonant with Christian understandings of the incarnation. It challenges the sharp division between sacred and secular that persists even within Christian frameworks. Any effort to reintegrate these spheres of human experience, he adds, is itself sacramental, in that it effects salvation.

This sacramental worldview has important implications for African American Catholic worship, Rivers claims—namely, that all aspects of creation can be channels of God's grace. In contrast to the God often projected in Christian ritual—one who requires reserve, decorum, and propriety—Black people have envisioned a God who is a lover of singing and dancing, of human expressiveness, of color and dress; a God who could create and delight in living beings. Worship that is truly human and truly Godlike, Rivers contends, requires a broad sensorium of engagement—visual, auditory, kinesthetic, and tactile—that reflects the "fertile genius" of God exhibited in creation.[19] For worship to be pleasing to the God of creation, the offering people make of themselves must reflect the dynamic "livingness" of the created world.

These perceptions confirm and expand the sacramental approach so central to Catholic worship, and invite communities to discover new dimensions of that heritage—so that not only actions with bread and wine, oil and water, but the whole aliveness of the event, as well as those who participate, will carry the sacramentality of the rite. Color, sound, movement, pulse, and rhythm, which reflect the energy and revelatory kenosis of God in creation, enhance liturgy's sacramentality, revealing a God who rejoices in the created universe and delights to be among God's own children.

Realizing God's Liberating Intentions—Worship and Biblical Faith

Rivers posits that Black Christians bring to worship a distinct theological perspective on the biblical narratives: one in which God's liberation is central.[20] This focus on liberation, which reverberates today in the renaissance of Black theology, has its roots in the vicissitudes

of slavery and the continued struggle of Black Americans for freedom and wholeness within the oppressive structures of American
society. Contrary to the common assumption that Christianity was
forced upon the enslaved foreparents of African Americans, Rivers
asserts that biblical religion spoke to their sense of justice and right
reason. For an enslaved people, deliverance in this world was a necessity—and the God they encountered in the biblical narratives was
one who heard their cries for help and acted on behalf of the oppressed. African American slaves saw themselves as "the children of
Israel," suffering under the yoke of oppression in Egypt—and they
were sure that "The Lord was good to Israel, and his ways don't ever
change!"[21] In Jesus, they found the "great Emancipator," a companion and guide in their struggle for justice and wholeness.

Over the last several centuries, Rivers contends, African American worship has been a primary place in which African Americans
have experienced God's liberation, both communal and personal.
Impelled by the biblical narratives, worship in the Black Church has
been a platform from which congregations have struggled against
oppression within the social and political arena. Moreover, Black
worship has created a space within which individuals could discover
self-esteem, could express their "somebodiness" in the face of the
negative messages of an oppressive society. Within the Black worship ideal, one can be free to "be oneself," to bring all dimensions of
one's humanness, to shed tears of both joy and sorrow, and to know
that "It's all right!" James Cone corroborates Rivers' insight, claiming that the experience of liberation is key to Black worship—the
"power of God's Spirit invading the lives of people, 'buildin' them
up where they are torn down and proppin' them up on every leanin'
side.'"[22] In worship, the divine Spirit who is the power of Jesus
"breaks into the lives of the people, giving them a new song to sing
as confirmation of God's presence with them in [their] struggle," and
freeing them with a redemptive empowerment that enables them to
be agents of God's justice in the world.

Emotion as a Way of Knowing the Other—the Basis of Communion

From the perspective of Black religious culture, emotion is a primary way of knowing. It is a means of spiritual, even mystical participation in worship[23] and essential to its effectiveness. Rivers decries the unfortunate but often-held notion that emotion is the enemy of thought and reason, a perception that has pervaded many Western religious traditions, causing them to be wary of feelings as anti-spiritual. Even Thomas Aquinas, he notes, viewed knowledge as an operation of the whole person and not of the mind alone.

Emotion, contends Rivers, is one of many ways that human persons know and relate to the world. It is a key way of apprehending the Other. Like all knowledge, it is ultimately motivated by reason. In contrast to classic European approaches to reason, which are primarily analytic, African philosopher Leopold Sedar Senghor describes Black African reason as intuitive, as desirous of sharing life with the Other.[24] Drawing on his insights, Rivers underscores that *e-motion* is just what the word implies: a moving out of oneself toward the Other that enables an intuitive sharing of life. Hence, it is the basis of any richly human communion. In worship, emotion is not a fall from consciousness but an accession to a higher state of knowing—a communion with the Other that Senghor likens to a love dance.

Rivers' perceptions here are echoed by several contemporary authors who play out the importance of emotion to the biblical Word proclaimed in liturgy and the ethical living it is meant to shape. "Feeling and emotion are an intrinsic part of revelation itself," states Nathan Mitchell. "God's word to us is not only cognitive and rational; it is incarnate and emotional."[25] Martha Nussbaum describes emotions as "upheavals of thought," as "judgments of value," as energies "suffused with intelligence and discernment" that are an integral part of people's systems of ethical judgment.[26] From these perspectives, emotion, expressed in the faith-communication that unfolds in worship, is formative of what Toinette Eugene describes as "orthopa-thy"—"righteous heart or feeling"—that can mediate between ortho-doxy, "right teaching," and orthopraxis, "right action."[27] Hence, the African American predilection for dramatic, soulful, and emotional engagement in worship can create a context for hearing the Word and putting it into practice.

The Worshiping Assembly as "Primary Witness of Faith"

A major purpose for which people assemble for worship, Rivers pos-its, is to witness to the faith that is in them in such a way that others are moved and inspired.[28] The primary witness of faith is hence the congregation, the participating assembly as a whole. In Black Church worship, he notes, testimony to one's faith, both verbal and gestural, is integral to the fabric of worship. The whole event is participatory, dialogic, and polyphonic. People contribute freely, affecting each other, building up each other's faith. Indeed, a silent, unresponsive congregation puts a damper on the whole event—on the effective-ness of the leadership and the community's ability to perceive the Spirit's movements—while the responsive assembly brings the wor-ship to its heights, and releases the dynamic leadership of those who minister.

Implicit in this practice, Rivers contends, is an understanding that the role of liturgical ministers is to unlock the assembly's capa-bilities to witness to their faith in an active way; to evoke rather than silence the response of others; and to enable persons to sing and pray with power and meaning. This inverts the often-held assump-tion that ministers play the primary role, "inspiring" the community through their words and gestures, acting on their behalf. Rather, Riv-ers proposes, people need to be invited to take their legitimate role as subjects of the action, and be empowered to do more than "stay in their places and do what is required." People must learn to partici-pate, just as actors learn their parts, and be given latitude to give witness to their faith. Reciprocally, people's faith testimony, as we noted in the Black Church, can unlock the best leadership that ministers can provide.

Gospel Metanoia as Catharsis—Worship and Spiritual Renewal

Catharsis is essential to metanoia, Rivers contends, to the deep renewal of sprit that worship is meant to effect.[29] True catharsis, he claims, carries people beyond momentary feelings of devotion to a more lasting commitment to Gospel discipleship. He finds models for such catharsis in three sources: biblical narratives describing the action of God's Spirit, the Black religious tradition, and effective theater.

In Genesis, the Spirit of God breathed over the waters, transforming them into life-sustaining, life-renewing bodies. The same wind-breath-Spirit enfleshed lifeless, dry bones in Ezekiel's account, and stirred the pool of Bethesda to release its healing powers. New birth, from a Johannine perspective, is effected by water-and-the-Spirit; and the pentecostal outpouring of the Spirit transformed timid disciples into courageous witnesses.

This biblical, Spirit-induced metanoia is paralleled in the experience of traditional Black Church worship. In fact, change for the better is the expected norm. People come to worship to be renewed—to leave worship refreshed and revived, inspired and healed. If weary spirits, burdened by physical and psychological strains, are not revived and revitalized, even moved to ecstacy,[30] "the Spirit was not present." Spirit-induced catharsis in worship, Rivers claims, was a primary means by which African Americans survived the oppression of slavery. Moreover, it has moved Black communities to a political and social activism that was powerfully demonstrated in the Civil Rights movement of the '60s.

Good theater likewise effects catharsis. Effective drama has the power to engage people affectively and intellectually in a redemptive perspective on the human condition; to invite them experientially into the deepest sufferings and most expansive joys of human living;

and to awaken, within the dramatic tension, a hope and expectation of a lasting transformation. This catharsis lasts well beyond the performance. It shapes people's perception of the world, and can motivate a new response in their everyday living.[31]

Such catharsis is integral to effective worship, Rivers holds. Despite a concerted effort at liturgical reform in Catholic practice, worship still often lacks the vitality and life that can effect the metanoia for which people hunger. The difficulty is not that the surrounding culture has become too materialistic, he contends, but that the worship of many churches is not spiritual enough—not imbued with the living vitality of the Spirit of God, who roots people in their human vocation, awakens them to Good News of the Gospel, and empowers them to be witnesses in the world. Enabling this Spirit to be experienced, as a means of revitalizing the worship of African American communities, requires that the drama of worship reach its goal, catharsis—a catharsis that insures that the emotional content of worship does not leave communities with momentary feelings of well-being, but moves them to deepening renewal. And this will require a creative use of our living tradition of worship, so as to engender an intentional framework within which the Spirit can be released.

Appropriating the "Living Tradition" Creatively

From an African American perspective, any performative tradition, be it ritual or artistic, must be received and handed on creatively if it is to remain living.[32] Otherwise, it will atrophy and die. Gospel songs, for example, are reinterpreted, so that new and creative ways of performing treasured pieces will keep the tradition alive and the faith memory living. They are interpreted to insure that they stay in the repertoire, so that their perennial message will be spoken to new generations and within new circumstances. Without originality and spontaneity, Rivers posits, inherited patterns and forms not only atrophy; they can "enslave" rather than free.[33]

From this perspective, Rivers maintains, to receive a tradition of worship—the rubrics, the forms and patterns, the structures—and hand it on without change is to render it without the living Spirit of God. The "rites" of Catholic practice may be well-structured theologically, he notes, but not performatively—that is, dramatically, artistically, rhetorically. The living art of worship needs breath and wings, creative tension and salvific resolution, newness and originality. As African American communities respond to the Spirit at work in their midst, he suggests, rubrical norms will need to be invitations to artistic response rather than recipes, points of departure for variation rather than fixed molds.[34] Knowing the tradition is essential; but receiving it with a discerning freedom will keep it alive for new generations.

In the rhythms and word-play of a sermon entitled "Worship in Spirit and Truth," Rivers situates this orientation toward a creative use of the tradition—which sets its sight on the future rather than on the past—in a biblical framework:

> We Roman Catholics . . . need a firm Roman Catholic foundation to stand on. We need an appropriate platform from which we can preview the future. But if the heritage from the past blinds us to that which is yet-to-be, so that we can see only what *has been*, our link with the movement of the Divine in Scripture is severed. In the Bible, while God is a God of history, of heritage, he is also the God who has his finger fixed on the future. The gaze of God in the book of the Bible is not on the Garden of Eden past, but to the bride come down from the heavens, and to the new city in the making![35]

Reclaiming the Predilections of an Oral Culture in a Worship Tradition Shaped by Ocularity

Of all the cultural-religious foundations Rivers lays out, this last is perhaps the most probing and the deepest challenge to interculturation. He notes that Catholic practice is deeply imbued with cultural, philosophical presuppositions quite different from those of Black culture; that its style, modality, and what is sometimes called its "genius"—brevity, terseness, objectivity, lack of redundancy, and, Rivers would add, discursiveness—inhibit the true engagement in, and enjoyment of, worship that will nourish the faith of African American communities.[36] Given the significance of this challenge, he explores it in some detail.

Rivers points out that Western Christianity has been deeply affected by a discursiveness and a "puritanism"[37] that are wary of emotion and enjoyment. From his perspective, this cultural thrust is the single greatest obstacle to effective, dramatic worship.[38] The roots of these tendencies, Rivers posits, are not religious but cultural. Traditional Western religions describe themselves as incarnational and sacramental, and Western mystics frequently image their involvement with the divine using sensual or sexual imagery. Yet an implicit "puritanism," which discredits the body and holds all that pleasurably stimulates the senses as suspect, is prevalent in Western religion precisely because it pervades much of Western culture. Fear of bodily and sensual engagement in worship is widespread, and with it a fear of emotion. Discursive liturgy is often equated with "a more spiritual" expression of worship.

This tendency, Rivers contends, is at root a "sight-based" cultural orientation. While claiming to be more *intellectual*, it is actually more *ocular*—that is, "of the eye." This ocular orientation, he proposes, developed in the West centuries before Plato articulated the bias in his hierarchy of the senses, a hierarchy in which sight is preeminent—lofty, ennobling, and spiritual—while touch and all things sensual are debasing and humanly degrading. Aristotle opens his *Metaphysics*, Rivers notes, with an affirmation that "of all the senses, trust only the sense of sight!" Thus he paved the way for a domination of Western culture by the rationalist assumptions that Descartes and others would formulate over the centuries. From this perspective, emotion is the enemy of thought, reason, perception, and understanding. Worship that is enjoyable or entertaining, that is filled with the emotional engagement typical of the traditional Black Church worship, is suspect and must be deplored in favor of a more "intellectual" approach. *by mat*

Rivers pursues this notion of an ocular orientation further. As human persons apprehend and know the world through the eye alone, they perceive a flat, continuous world—without rhythm, without interval, without interface, and without a third dimension that only touch can discern. The eye perceives a continuing line, sensing continuity in all it sees whether or not the objects viewed are connected. Touch, on the other hand, discovers intervals and spaces—it delights in discontinuity and rhythm. The eye focuses on one thing at a time, abstracting it from its context, distinguishing and analyzing what it sees, and in so doing, separating conceptually what is not in fact separate. Ultimately, ocularity favors detached, uninvolved observation—needing distance from what is perceived in order to apprehend it.

Rivers notes that African-based cultures, in contrast, are oral, aural, and poetic in orientation. They are sound-based cultures in which poetry is preferred to literal truth, rhetoric and dramatic communication to scientific discourse. In oral-aural cultures, all the senses are required for apprehending and knowing the world. The eye is not dominant, but functions integrally with all the other senses. "There is a natural tendency for interpenetration and interplay, creating a concert or orchestration in which the ear sees, the eye hears, and where one both smells and tastes color, wherein all the senses, unmuted engage in every experience."[39] The world is perceived not through distance but through engagement—a reaching out to take hold of, to feel, to taste, to hear. There is no hesitance to become emotionally involved with what is perceived—since the demand for distance and detachment results from a dominance of the eye. Emotion, as we noted before, is an essential way of knowing, of engaging with the Other, of communion. Quoting Leopold Senghor, Rivers notes, "In contrast to Descartes' 'I think, therefore I am,' a Black African perception might be summarized, 'I am, I dance the other.' . . . In Black Africa, you dance because you feel. And to dance is a verb with precisely that object-complement; you never dance without dancing something or someone. Now, to dance is to uncover reality, to re-create, to fill one's being with vital force, to live a fuller life, to BE, which, after all, is the highest mode of knowing."[40]

Rivers parallels his distinction between ocular and oral cultures with the musical preferences evident in each. He posits that persons shaped by an ocular, linear orientation tend to be melodically oriented, and generally less sophisticated in matters of rhythm—precisely because rhythm is created by breaking the continuity in a musical line. In contrast, African American music, based in the predilections of oral culture, is rhythmically generated, favoring complex and polyrhythmic structures that create a discontinuity in the musical line. This break in the musical line prompts reciprocal, rhythmic movements in the human body. The bias of Western liturgical traditions toward ocular culture, and its concomitant favoring of melodically generated music, has led to a degrading of rhythmic music on moral grounds. Rivers references a document from the Federation of Diocesan Liturgical Commissions circulating at the time of his writing[41] that stated that music with "an emphasis on beat [elicits] physical, impulsive and unconscious involvement." In contrast, music with "melodic emphasis . . . leads the listener inwardly to an attitude of interior reflection." "Beat music," the document continues, establishes a style of worship that highlights its "horizontal or humanistic" dimensions, while "melody music" elicits a worship style that is more "vertical or spiritually elevating." The implied message is that the latter provides a sounder theological basis for liturgical action. This prejudicial view degrades rhythmically generated music, an intrinsic characteristic of most African American music, as unserious at best and theologically deficient at worst; and it privileges those styles of worship that may enlighten the mind but may be less able to move the heart.

The challenge of interculturation, Rivers proposes, is not to dismiss the orientations of Western culture, with its thrust toward more detached, discursive, and technological approaches, but to recognize that all people need both the discursive and the poetic.[42] Communities shaped by the contrasting Western and African-based ideals have much to learn from each other. However, he maintains, the pro-detachment, pro-discursive bias of Western culture, which tends to be antipoetic, antiartistic, and antiemotional, seriously inhibits the kind of engagement necessary for effective religious celebration, especially in African American communities. As these communities recover the art of dramatically expressive and emotionally involved worship, they invite the larger Catholic community to relearn the "art of celebration", lest it lose a sense of transcendence through a preoccupation with the analytic modes of science and technology. The fruit of this exchange will be more than a learning of new "techniques of performance." Rather, it will enable persons and communities to be more effective witnesses to their faith, freer channels of God's grace and the Spirit's action in Christian worship.

A Performative Approach to Effective Worship: Dramatic Structure and Artistic Performance

Having laid out several of the cultural-religious foundations that ground Rivers' approach, we turn now to his performative view of worship.[43] Rivers is clear: effective worship is ultimately dependent on the Spirit of God. But it is facilitated by two dynamics—discerning the *dramatic structure* of a whole worship event, and insuring the *artistic performance* of each of its elements. Both are necessary if the catharsis that opens the way for the Spirit's action is to happen.

Dramatic structure is not simply a given, Rivers contends, inherent in the liturgical rites as presented in Catholic ritual books. These may have theological, historical, and rubrical coherence, but they beg the performative question: how will worship effect metanoia in the lives of those engaged? Often, he notes, worship events lack organic unity. Even memorable parts lose their impact because the worship *as a whole* lacks the "dramatic structure" that could render the experience moving and effective. What is missing is a performative understanding of how the whole liturgy comes to have unity, coherence, and emphasis. What is lacking is an effective structure that could insure that the event is not static but has movement, flow, and direction—one part flowing into the other—since movement signals an aliveness that can "attract and hold the attention, absorb the hearer or [engage] the viewer, making 'renewal' possible."[44]

Dramatic structure, Rivers posits, is the fruit of sensitive and discerning planning. It requires a responsive approach, on the part of those who prepare worship, to how a particular celebration takes on coherent form—based on the Word of God to be proclaimed; the call and challenge it addresses to the community at this moment in their lives; and how the preaching, prayer, and music can flow from the Word and shape the ritual action. It requires choices based on an artistic sense of the performative impact of each element of the worship; for example, recognizing the difference between a *needless* repetition of elements—intercessions occurring at multiple points in the service—and the *necessary* repetition that creates emotional and dramatic intensity within the liturgy—multiple repetitions of a song or hymn refrain, each building the performative intensity. This kind of discerning planning will recognize that the "logic" of a rite as laid out in a liturgical book may inhibit the ritual movement suggested by the scriptures on a particular occasion. For example, a strong Gospel call to repentance might suggest that a "penitential rite" at the opening of the service is premature, and would be considerably more effective after the homily. Ultimately, the goal of this performative approach to structure is not to make light of the tradition or its ritual patterns—clearly it requires both competence and a knowledge of the tradition—but to enable the worship event as a whole to facilitate the Spirit's action, to evoke catharsis and invite metanoia. The spontaneity, naturalness, and élan that awaken people's hearts to God's living breath are the fruit of careful and wise planning, Rivers contends, not its antithesis.[45]

Dramatic structure requires its "counter-axis," artistic performance. Sensitive preparation alone cannot release a community's faith witness or nourish people with God's recreative Word. It must be complemented by artistic performance, which, from Rivers' point of view, is the dynamic work of an entire assembly. It is a communal art, a learned ability to engage in worship at a level of excellence, soulfulness, and expressiveness that enables the Spirit to touch people's hearts and create change. The artistic performance of a community and its leaders "brings order out of chaos, changes the prosaic to the poetic, breathes life and soul into a dead text."[46] It rests not only in *what* is done but *how*—not only the content of the worship event, but the "art" of prayer-filled communication that takes place. This "learned art" involves a readiness to make room for spontaneity and interaction—a sensing when to linger, to dwell longer or to quicken the pace of the worship, allowing the conventional patterns of the liturgy to remain supple, fluid, and responsive. It requires a willingness to yield to moments of emotional intensity that emerge in the flow of the event. For African American communities, moments of such intensity are often bearers of catharsis and spiritual renewal that allow persons to feel the potency of the Spirit's presence, a deepening solidarity with the community, and an intimacy with God. Within Black worship, such moments are cultivated as a means of experiencing God's liberation and healing, of breathing in the recreative breath of the Spirit, and of discovering that even in troubled times, "God is my all and all."

The spoken word is key to artistic performance, Rivers contends, especially for African American communities.[47] The problem with much Catholic worship is not that it is too verbal, but that its words are too prosaic to carry the renewing breath of the Spirit. Like drama and poetry—which attempt to transcend the limitations of everyday speech, to express the thoughts of one's heart, to utter the unutterable and express the inexpressible—the words of prayer must do the same. "They must give heavenbent wings to the heavy thoughts that anchor our hearts to the ground."[48] The abstract theological precision of prayers in the Roman Sacramentary, Rivers comments, need more than to be well delivered. They simply lack the poetic strength that can move people's hearts. Their lack of poetry contributes to an "aesthetic incoherence" in the worship, in which prayers become "dead spots" rather than critical elements that propel the liturgy forward, that reach out for what is beyond, and move those gathered to the work of discipleship. In contrast, the patterns and energy of African American oratory provide a different model. No American who has heard Dr. Martin Luther King's address before the Lincoln Memorial, Rivers notes, can miss the power of his words. "I have a dream"—repeated over and again with intoxicating effect—carried listeners to the same "mountain top" from which they could see, with him, "the promised land." Long after Dr. King's death, these words continue to capture a vision that inspires and moves people to works of justice and equality.[49]

Music is likewise key to effective and artistic performance. As a communal art, as a carrier of soul, as capable of affecting the whole dramatic flow of the worship, music has the power to create an atmosphere within which true anamnesis can take place.[50] "Music, like its other self, poetry, seems capable of doing what plain rational words cannot do: namely, to express the unexpressible, to touch [people's] hearts, penetrate their souls [and] create an experience of things that cannot be reasoned."[51] In the words of an old African American adage, "The Spirit does not descend without song." Music adds depth, weight, breadth, and power to words that otherwise might remain unmemorable, Rivers contends. It can affect the dramatic flow of the service, or create the "atmosphere" of a particular moment in the liturgy. For example, singing the "Gospel acclamation" in a eucharistic liturgy ought to be as a "standing ovation to greet the Word of the Gospel," providing intensity and "magnitude" to the moment.

In traditional Black churches, Rivers points out, the whole assembly is essential to musical performance. Solo/choral singing or instrumental performance are never ends in themselves, but always intended to engage others, to draw them into a dynamic exchange of musical and spiritual energy, and to bring to expression the community's witness of faith. People feel free to respond, to interject their shouts and acclamations, and to sing along even in the midst of a solo performance. In the context of Black worship, music that is not soulful, that does not touch hearts, release spiritual power, and evoke a response within the community is simply not good music. Here, Rivers underscores the "functional aesthetic" that permeates all African American performance traditions, artistic and ritual—never *l'art pour l'art*, never for its own sake.[52] Rather, music in Black worship is meant to *do* something, to have an effect: to touch, encourage, inspire, and challenge people; and to create bonds of love and mutuality within the worshiping community.

Rivers contends that the "sophisticated art forms" of Black worship have much to teach communities about worship as a communal faith witness that invites metanoia.[53] Three arts are central—preaching, prayer, and song—respectively the "heart," the "strength," and the "soul" of Black worship.[54] Each carries high expectations of the skill and artistry of those who take leadership; each is rooted in a holistic performance aesthetic in which all art forms are dynamically interrelated. Black preaching often involves song, drama, poetry, and testimony; and Gospel singing is intensified through expressive movement and rhythmic dance. Spirituality is at the heart of this performance aesthetic, Rivers notes—a belief in the power of the Spirit to act through the one who sings or preaches—as well as a sacramental view of God's creative energy at work in those who worship. To perform is to release spiritual power, to invite others to taste transcendence.[55] The entire assembly is essential to this process; their responsive encouragement and affirmation, their demand for excellence and creativity, unlock the power of the prayer, the preaching, or the music.

In Black prayer and preaching, the use of the English language reaches its zenith.[56] Rivers describes preaching as "intellectual content infused by soul, by a spirit that has power to move and evoke . . . emotion."[57] A Black preacher's use of word-play, rhyme, alliteration, and poetry, coupled with a dramatic style, and his or her movement through an expected "three-fold progression" from ordinary speech, to chanting, to moments of ecstatic speech,[58] are all in the service of releasing the Spirit's action. The preacher intends to evoke the community's response, their interjections and Amens, their expressions of approval and affirmation, so as to build up and heighten the community's engagement with the Word. What is feared as a "disabling enemy," Rivers notes, is "the deadly silence of an unresponsive congregation."[59]

Black praying, likewise, requires poetry and transcendent language, a knowledge of traditional prayer patterns that are infused with spontaneity and deep sincerity. The affective and affecting power of words is cultivated in both Black preaching and prayer, not as a fascination with the subtleties of oral communication, but through a heightened sense that words are meant to have emotional impact. *How* the prayer or preaching is delivered is as important as the quality and poetic strength of the words spoken—since creating a felt-connection with those who hear, and evoking their Amens, are essential to how God is praised and the community is built up in faith. Rivers worked diligently to develop models for accessing Black modes of prayer and preaching and fusing them with the structures and purposes of Catholic liturgy.[60] The fruit of this effort can be sensed in the cadence and word-play of portions of a eucharistic prayer that he composed, and that is appended to this chapter.

Finally, music, the soul of Black worship, is as essential as prayer or preaching.[61] Music is never seen to interrupt or "hold up" the service, but shapes and nuances the unfolding liturgy. Rivers posits that the hallmarks of music in the African American tradition are creativity and freedom. Creativity is evident in the earliest shaping of Black music in the United States, forged during slavery, which involved a synthesis of African traditions—pulsing rhythms and interlocking call-response melodies—and the hymnody of Protestant Christian Churches. This creative tradition continues today, as new syntheses such as Rivers' own compositions are generated. Ultimately, Rivers contends, freedom is the most distinguishing feature of Black music. "Notice," he remarks, "how freely a good jazz instrumentalist revels and rhapsodizes even within the confines of a set rhythm. Notice how a good blues, gospel, or jazz singer can liberate the words of a text from the imprisonment of a given notation. . . . When music is free, it is soulful at its source, and soul-stirring in its effect. When music is free, it is alive, and communicates life."[62] This attribute of music, this freedom, becomes in worship a context for God's liberating action within the performing community—be it through tears, testimony, expressive movement, or spontaneous thanksgiving—inviting those caught up in the performance dynamic to experience themselves as "a child of God," as God's unique and intentional creation.

These arts of Black worship can inform, enrich, and revitalize the worship of African American Catholics, Rivers proposes. Together they hold out standards of artistic performance, as well as understandings of participation and mutual "inspiration," that can enable communities to embody their liturgy with dignity, grace, competence, and a keen sense of the mystery of God alive in the midst of God's people. Moreover, they each contribute to what Rivers has enumerated as the requirements of effective worship—that it nourish people's need for transcendence; that it address the concrete needs and concerns of a community; that it evoke a change of heart—a metanoia that leads to discipleship—and, finally, that it is truly enjoyable, filled with the élan of a people spiritually renewed and replete with a promise of God's present and future shalom.

The Salience of Rivers' Vision for the Contemporary Church

Having laid out the manifold dimensions of Rivers vision, we turn now to its salience for the contemporary Church. When Rivers' second volume, *The Spirit in Worship,* was published in 1978, Black and white theologians and liturgists heralded his work.[63] "Rivers has engraved the sacred seal of Blackness even more lucidly into liturgical theory and practice," wrote Bishop James Lyke. Rivers' "poetry and prose combine to produce a fervent intellectual instrument of hope and power for the people called Roman Catholics," commented Joseph R. Washington, Jr. Rivers' message, "in its humane-ness and in its frank appeal to the total person, [is] what the doctor should order for our dry, rationalistic and surfeited spirits," remarked Robert Hovda. Almost thirty years later, how might we assess the impact of his work and its significance for the contemporary Church? Let me offer several observations.

First, the scope of Rivers' vision of a fully inculturated Black Catholic liturgy was remarkable for his time. In asserting that for Black Catholics to reclaim their rightful heritage, the *whole* of Catholic liturgy must be suffused with their religious intuitions and cultural predilections, Rivers charted a course that would not be articulated by inculturation theorists until the 1980s and early 1990s.[64] He recognized, intuitively, that a simple insertion of cultural elements into established Catholic rites must give way to a deeper integration of worldviews; that a limited adaptation of ritual forms must yield to their more thorough transformation.[65] Moreover, he named what would only be voiced by inculturation theorists a decade later: that the rites of Catholic liturgy are already deeply inculturated—shaped by historical exigencies as carriers of European American cultural-religious assumptions. Rivers believed that to address the implications of these dispositions and biases, especially in what he judged to inhibit effective worship, was critical for the life of the Church and its mission. He offered his insights, trusting they would be received as part of a two-way dialogue—that distinctive cultural groups both receive *and* transform the larger tradition, enriching it with their gifts *and* critiquing its limitations and cultural shortsightedness.[66]

Perhaps Rivers' unique gift to understandings of inculturation has been his performative approach to liturgy—a practice-oriented, holistic strategy for how the spatial/temporal environment of worship, its inherent ritual structure, and varied performative expressions might be transformed from within, releasing newness and divine energy. In proposing such a method, Rivers remained focused on the ultimate purpose of worship: to effect God's salvation in Christ. His dramatic, performative, and artistic agenda is consistently at the service of worthy praise of God, human liberation, and effective mission. With this as the heart of the matter, the plethora of liturgical variations that might emanate from the process he proposed is grounded in the very heart of the Church's vocation.[67]

Second, at its release, *The Spirit in Worship* was hailed by Black scholar Joseph R. Washington, Jr., as a "liturgical *tour de force* . . . demanding that black life and culture be integrated at the heart of [Roman Catholic] worship and mission." But, he queried, can Rivers' "Roman Catholic brothers and sisters immerse themselves in the spirit from which breaks forth the black spirit in worship?"[68] The answer is, clearly, yes. Three decades later, Rivers' vision has been realized in a revitalized Catholic worship that flourishes in many African American communities around the country. A recent in-depth ethnographic study of one parish—Our Lady of Lourdes, San Francisco—reveals an assembly imbued with a cultural acumen, ritual resourcefulness, and liberating creativity that echoes Rivers' best hopes.[69] Although their practice is not directly attributable to his influence, his writings offer invaluable hermeneutical tools for interpreting their worship.[70]

In the late '70s, Rivers expressed a concern that African American communities that had embraced their heritage with some fullness might lose their Catholicity in their search for Blackness.[71] Today, his concern might be otherwise. As leadership in the Roman Church becomes more focused on "Catholic identity"—which at times is interpreted in terms of greater ritual, rubrical, and doctrinal conformity than was the case in the immediate decades after Vatican II—efforts may be brought to bear to restrict or uproot the initiatives already in place in African American communities to restore the fullness of their "Black *and* Catholic identity." To these communities, Rivers' vision remains a beacon, to stay the course and continue the necessary work of interculturation.

Third, "Everything Clarence Rivers affirms about the hunger of black communities for 'effective, affective worship' describes my own deepest desire," stated liturgist John Gallen in 1978. "This yearning hunger is not only black, not only mine . . . but characterizes the majority of the white community. If this is true, it makes the root insight of this book endlessly significant for liturgy in more churches than black ones."[72] As Gallen recognized, Rivers' work implicitly called for an intercultural dialogue that would wrestle with the common hungers for spiritual renewal that mark the whole American Church. That dialogue has yet to be realized, although its potential has not lessened with time.

For example, Rivers underscored that living traditions require creativity and renewal if they are not to atrophy and die; that local communities must constantly make connections between their cultural worlds and the Christian mystery, discerning how the Spirit is at work, and shaping liturgical practice accordingly. Today, as retrenchment, a new rubricism, and a recentralization of authority and liturgical control emerge in Catholic practice, threatening, it would seem, the ongoing renewal envisioned by Vatican II, can Rivers' vision be received as timely wisdom and prophetic challenge? Likewise, within such an intercultural dialogue, undertaken in mutuality and love, can Rivers' appraisal of Western cultural orientations, such as ocularity and discursiveness—which reside deeply within the collective psyche of many Catholic worshipers—be received with openness? Can the invitation to a deeper sharing of cultural wisdom, which he holds out to the larger Church, be realized? Can the insights of Black religious culture be welcomed as healing balm and ritual wisdom for the whole Church?

Finally, Rivers' work demonstrates the invaluable contribution that African American liturgists and theologians have made to both scholarship and Church life over the past several decades. Yet their vision and experience continue to be marginalized.[73] How can the gifts they bring be more fully welcomed? How can a healing dialogue be created that will help lead the Church into the future of its worship traditions? Rivers' own words, preached in a sermon he entitled "Worship in Spirit and Truth," sum up the challenge:

> The church must not allow the brilliant glory of her traditional and familiar worship forms to blind her to other possibilities, to prevent her from appropriating with appreciation a new vitality within her midst, a vitality, a life, new to her, but conceived long ago in the ancient and fertile womb of Mother Africa. . . . Even so, a people who once were enslaved are now the channels of the freeing and renewing Spirit. . . . [But] let not the Black presence within the church become wrapped up in itself, but continue to press the offering of that dimension of the abundant life with which it has been particularly endowed. [74]

Excerpts from a Eucharistic Prayer,
Composed in the Tradition of Black Prayer,
by Clarence R. J. Rivers

O God of heaven and earth / with grateful and uplifted hearts,
with grateful and with heartfelt praise,
bound—obliged by joy-filled thankfulness, / we come before thee,
worshiping in spirit and in truth, / having drunk from thy cup
so full of goodness that it overflows, / having been protected by the
      arms
of thy goodness and thy mercy / that have—like a mother's love—
followed, looked after, and embraced us / all the days of our lives. . . .
Mothering and Fathering, / thou has set a spiritual table
around which we, thy scattered, exiled, / wandering and lonely
      children might be gathered
to recognize each other in / the Breaking of the Bread.
Gathered thus into thy family circle / basking in the warmth of so
      much love
made known to us in Jesus Christ, / feeling like Ezekiel's new nation
with the Spirit and the Soul renewed in us, / newborn again of water
      and the Spirit
with hearts of stone made into hearts of flesh, / our thankfulness
      wells up
into a song of praise / to glorify thy works for endless days . . .
O holy God, holy mighty one, holy immortal one, . . . we thank you
      because:
before the curtain of time had risen / you stepped out upon the stage
      of nothingness
you spoke the words wherewith worlds were formed; / you spoke
      your lines
and the drama of heaven and earth came into being; /
you stooped down low and scooped up clay from the river's edge,—
shaped [humankind]—/ breathed into our nostrils of clay the Spirit
      of life; /

so now we live and move and have our being,
have the dynamism of your Spirit / have the power of Soul.
We thank you that one day you dispatched from glory / your darling
   Son, Jesus Christ . . .
that he might walk our walk, and talk our talk, /
and grant to each of us a right to the tree of life. /
We thank you for having taken your seat among the downtrodden,
   the dehumanized,
the dispossessed, the denounced, / and the denied people of the
   universe . . .
Thank you, Lord of justice and righteousness, / for you heard our
   cries,
pitied every groan . . . put our feet on freedom's path, /
and told us even as you told Lot . . . not to look back. . . .
We confess, the path of freedom has not been an easy one; . . .
sometimes, in the desert of our wanderings, / we have preferred . . .
   false security
to the responsibilities of freedom and liberation.
Have mercy, we pray, upon us in our moments of weakness. . . .
Lord God, we thank you, / that even in our darkest hour,
even when the midnight hour of despair is upon us, / you keep hope
   alive. . . .
Singing with faith and with hope, facing the rising sun of a new day
   begun,
somehow we find the strength to march on, / knowing that we shall
   overcome.
And now, thou font of every blessing, / whose spirit makes
   everything alive,
even as we are gathered around your holy table, / remembering the
   upper room,
breathe upon these offerings and let them become the body and
   blood

of Jesus Christ, our Lord, / who has called us to celebrate this great
    mystery. . . .

Even as we, your thankful children / remember the wonderful works
    of thy salvation,
made manifest in Jesus Christ, / even so remember us when your
    kingdom comes;
let us be counted in that blessed number, / when the saints go
    marching in.
And so that we may enter into your kingdom, / where none may
    enter
that is not new-born again, . . . / refresh our lives with the water of
    your Spirit,
even as we are nourished time and again / by the body of Christ
    Jesus.
Refresh the life of your church . . . / let the Soul, the Spirit of Jesus,
keep alive his every member. . . . / Let the Pentecostal flame burn
    bright
upon . . . all the pastors of your flock. / Give your people arms of
    spiritual power
to lift too-heavy loads from one another's / sometimes overburdened,
    hurting backs. . . .
Finally, Father, when it is yours to call and we must answer,
may we be found faithful to every trust placed in our hands.
May we look back on a life well spent in your service,
and look forward to a joyful day that has no end.
We look forward to the morning of that great resurrection,
when all the dead shall rise / even as your Son, our brother and
    savior, Jesus Christ.
Through Him, with Him, in Him . . .[75]

PART THREE   AESTHETIC PRINCIPLES

Constructing an African American Catholic Liturgical Aesthetic

Ronald D. Harbor

The purpose of this chapter is to identify the characteristic features of an African American Catholic liturgical aesthetic—that is, understandings of what is beautiful, sacred, praiseworthy, profoundly expressive, and life-giving—that might guide the lived practice of worshiping communities now and into the future.[1] This liturgical aesthetic, mediated through a lexicon of performative values, draws on the pastoral and theological ferment of Black scholarship over the past several decades, and most particularly the generative work of the first Black Catholic Theological Symposium in 1978.

As demonstrated in the preceding chapter, the vision of Father Clarence R. J. Rivers has been pivotal in shaping a framework for effective worship that remains a beacon for African American communities and potentially for the larger Church. This chapter puts Father Rivers' work in conversation with that of three other Black Catholic scholars—Doctor Toinette Eugene, Bishop Edward Kenneth Braxton,[2] and Father Glenn Jean-Marie—all of whom addressed the 1978 Black Catholic Theological Symposium.[3] Taken together, the anthropological, catechetical, theological, and liturgical insights of these leaders provide a foundation for explicating a set of twenty-three performative values that might serve African American communities as they continue to forge life-giving expressions of Catholic worship. Moreover, the liturgical aesthetic I construct here, rooted in the rich soil of Black life and spirituality, illuminates the distinctive gift of Black Catholics to the multicultural tapestry of lived faith in the American Church, and might serve as a model for a similar discernment of performative values appropriate to other cultural communities.

While much development has taken place in Black Catholic theology since the 1978 symposium, I return to this starting point, to this first arduous striving on the part of African American scholars to name, claim, and articulate Black Catholic life lived at full stretch before God, because I believe the depths of insights contained here have yet to be fully plumbed in a way that utilizes them in a fully realized expression of Black Catholic worship.[4] The presentations of the four scholars we will explore underscore the distinctiveness and value of constructing an African American aesthetic for Roman Catholic worship. Moreover, I believe that the work of these and other scholars at the symposium contains a nascent sacramental theology that begs for a more prolonged discernment and careful scrutiny than can be given in this short chapter.

An African American aesthetic in Roman Catholic liturgy was considered an anomaly in 1956,[5] the year Father Clarence R. J. Rivers began to ponder how to imbue the Roman rite with the spiritual legacy and cultural genius of the African American community. His earliest efforts to plumb this relationship were almost unknown outside his parish, St. Joseph's Catholic Church, a predominately African American assembly in Cincinnati, Ohio. Yet his liturgical insight gained national attention in 1964 when, at the first Mass in English held at the annual Liturgical Conference in St. Louis, he introduced his composition, "God is Love." With that single song, the seeds of a cultural-liturgical revolution were planted within the larger Catholic community.[6]

While not inciting a revolution, Rivers' introduction of music of "particular ethnic origin"[7] aided a fledgling articulation of Black

Catholic concerns regarding Catholic worship. In some settings, as noted in Part One, it engendered an array of liturgical innovations that reflected the religious worldview of African Americans. In 1978, Father Rivers joined other Black scholars and pastoral leaders to forge a cogent discourse on Black theology. The proceedings of this first Black Catholic Theological Symposium, later published as *Theology: A Portrait in Black*,[8] represent a corporately constructed, interdisciplinary theological-cultural framework for releasing and cultivating the gifts of Black Catholics in the Roman Church.

The 1978 symposium gave initial impetus to the formulation of an African American "aesthetical distillate"[9]—one that is grounded in the Roman Catholic tradition yet reaches beyond the Western European philosophical approach. For this reason, the insights of scholars who participated in that gathering hold such importance for the honing of authentic Black Catholic worship today. Together they addressed the need for: (1) an integration of African and American Catholic philosophical concerns in the articulation of a Black Catholic spiritual-cultural ethos; (2) the validation of a Black American and Black Catholic worldview that would inform the pastoral care of African American communities; (3) a probing of the negative effects of an inappropriate catechesis of Black Catholics and subsequent research into methodological correctives;[10] (4) a search for sources of Black wisdom and the incorporation of these insights into theological investigation; and (5) a fuller vision of justice and the ethical welfare of African Americans, especially Black Catholics, in both civil and ecclesial spheres.

All of these concerns inform the work of this chapter—constructing an African American Catholic liturgical aesthetic mediated through a set of theologically based performative values that can be placed at the service of Catholic worship. The scholarship distilled in *Theology: A Portrait in Black* underscores that all aspects of African American cultural-religious life must come to bear on how communities shape their worship. Moreover, it implies that Black Catholics must continually discern the appropriateness of liturgical directives and ritual rubrics that ignore or minimize their cultural legacy and spiritual quests.

The sections that follow examine the insights of four of the symposium scholars, identifying the distinctive perspective each offers to the task at hand. Their presentations make clear the enormous complexity of naming and claiming the theological foundations for a lived liturgical aesthetic.

Doctor Toinette Eugene: "Developing Black Catholic Belief: Catechesis as a Black Articulation of Faith"

Invited to speak to the 1978 symposium on catechesis in the African American community, Dr. Toinette Eugene[11] challenged participants to name and reclaim the story of Black Catholics through the ministry of catechesis.[12] While faith-formation rather than worship was her primary focus, she alluded several times throughout her presentation to the reciprocity between catechesis and liturgy.[13] It is my contention that the agenda she spells out for Black catechesis finds a parallel in the aesthetic requirements of authentic and fully realized Black Catholic liturgy. Her work is pertinent to our task of constructing a liturgical aesthetic for several reasons: (1) she emphasizes that the formation of both the worshiping community and its ministers is essential to effective liturgy; (2) the spiritual heritage and quests that inform the content and methodology of the catechesis she envisions are likewise those that lead to authentic Black Catholic worship; and (3) her claim that a Black articulation of Catholic faith is essential for catechesis is instructive for constructing a lexicon of performative values for African American Catholic communities.

Eugene states categorically that Black catechesis must be rooted in Black experience—a contention, she argues passionately, that has not been the assumption of most of the Church's leadership. She roots this perception in the centrality of the Word of God to the task of catechesis. The Word of God, she states, determines both the content and the form of catechesis—defining its *content* as a proclamation of events, not ideas or precepts; and underscoring its *form* as Revelation, that is, as Good News! Hence for African American people, "God's revelation of [Godself] and the [Good News of the] redemptive mission of Jesus can only fully occur in the context in which Black people can perceive God's presence and action in their lives,"[14] that is, in their Black experience.

Eugene's view of a catechesis articulated from the Black experience has several salient features: first of all, it "gathers an entire Christian community . . . in a participatory experience of deepening maturity in the faith," while "utilizing and leaning upon God's gracious Word and Presence . . . as revealed in the midst of Black struggle, survival, and success." It seeks to build up the believing community as persons who "collectively profess the Lordship of Jesus Christ, . . . accept the liberating presence of God's Holy Spirit," and embrace the call to participate prophetically "in the transformation of the Church's institutions and the renewal of all peoples."[15] This rich vision of catechesis, as described by Eugene, might well find a parallel in a vision of fully realized Catholic worship.

Key to Eugene's vision is a call for the *indigenization* of catechesis in the Black Catholic community. Historically, African American Catholics have been denied all three dimensions of a true indigenization: that is, the establishment of a self-ministering, self-sustaining, and self-propagating faith community.[16] Yet although racist and sexist exclusionary policies have historically denied many available and competent Black Catholic ministers a role in Church leadership,[17] this has not negated the current availability of Black persons who have competence and charism to interpret the Word of God for African American communities. These nonordained spokespersons must be prepared to lead the way, Eugene contends, as sensitive and informed leaders for a new generation.[18] Only then can "the Black Catholic community articulate for itself and for the larger Church how and why and when the Good News has been an incomparable model and paradigm for its own striving toward liberation from situations of dehumanizing oppression."[19]

It is within the framework of such a truly indigenous catechesis that individuals and communities can be supported in their growth toward mature faith: that is, in their ability to recognize "what the Gospel and liberation mean in their lives"; "how justice and peace as Christian virtues become their own expression of Gospel living"; and what the "poverty, anger, frustration, and suffering [they experience] mean while responding to God in their own circumstances."[20] Catechesis, evangelization, religious formation, and, we might add, liturgy "must start where Revelation begins for Black people—in their own specific culture and ethos."

Eugene contends that a truly African American catechesis will lead to the transformation of the symbols of faith—that is, the stories of scripture and the rituals of the Church—once these have been interpreted from the perspective of Black experience. Although white Church leaders have rarely looked to Black symbols and signs as either instructive or appropriate, Black stories of death and new life, Black rituals as performed within a Black community centered on Jesus, are not only enlightening and powerful, but are valuable expressions of authentic Christian faith and catechesis. The incorporation of these faith documents in catechesis and in worship will create a transformative experience for Black communities who will now feel welcomed to the table of life in the Church, not as second-class citizens but as true children of God and agents of their own mature faith. Moreover, Eugene contends, quoting Alfred North Whitehead, without this transformation of symbol, the Church's faith communication is in danger of great loss: "Societies which cannot combine reverence for symbols with freedom of revision must ultimately decay either from anarchy or from slow atrophy."[21]

Black catechesis is rooted in Black theology, which "articulates the significance of Black Christian presence in an always oppressive white world"[22] The task of Black theology, Eugene notes, is to "analyze the Black condition in light of God's revelation in Jesus Christ," in order to create a new understanding of Black dignity and Black identity among African American people. Black theology "lifts up the reality of Black experience as relevant to the theological task" and "places the actions of Black people toward liberation in the Christian perspective, with Christ as model for participation in Black struggle for freedom." Rooted in Black theology, catechesis shapes an African American self-consciousness that associates Black self-identity with "Biblical liberation and God's identification with the oppressed." Moreover, it requires a "commitment to God's mission in the world revealed in Christ as liberating love." It is truly this liberating love that has the power to transform the often negative meanings associated with the term "Black"—such as darkness, evil, emptiness, void—into "positive images for identity." It places "emphasis on the liberative, celebrative, and life-affirming character of Christian faith." It is no wonder, therefore, that Eugene can state confidently that "good catechesis articulated from Black experience ought to lead to a great liturgical expression around the table of the Lord!" Moreover, she adds, liturgy well celebrated contributes to the vital work of catechesis: the "language of participatory prayer, Black music, poetry, and Black sermons must play a crucial part in continuing Black articulation of Christian faith expressed as catechesis!"

Eugene concludes that a "truly Black articulation within evangelization, catechesis, and religious education"—and, we might add, liturgy—"is crucial to the religious survival of that community. It is also essential to the mature faith development of the larger Catholic community of the Church."[23] In summarizing the essentials and sources for an effective Black catechesis, she underscores several key dimensions of liturgical practice:

1. *"There is a need for stressing the primacy of the Black experience,"* understanding that "'Black experience' is not monolithic." This

is the "point of departure," the "the source for training religious leaders and catechists," because it relates the situation of African American people to the biblical Word and to ongoing revelation.

2. "*The knowledge of Black history, religious and secular, is essential for those who lead and teach in the Black Catholic community*," because it displays "the determination of a people who would be liberated from all oppression."

3. "*The development of Black culture is an essential element to be expressed within the content of Black catechesis.*" Culture is critical, because it "shapes the ethos of a people . . . forms and reflects [their] values . . . determines a people's notions about the purpose of life . . . and the role of the Transcendent in life. It is the natural foundation on which religion must be built. Consequently, successful . . . catechesis within the Black community can only begin with a basic reference, respect, and knowledge of that culture."

4. "*Revelation needs to be stressed as an essential source for a Black articulation in catechesis*"—revelation seen as "what God is doing every day in human history on behalf of oppressed people." Scripture, the "quintessential aspect of Revelation," reveals "Jesus Christ and His resurrection event," and hence is the "clue and key" to catechesis in the Black experience.

5. "*Working in a Church structure bound by tradition, the use of tradition as a freeing element for a Black Catholic catechesis must be creative.*" Tradition "refers first and foremost to the theological reflection of the Church upon the nature of *all* Christianity, from the time of the early Church until now. It did not begin with the Council of Trent." However, "the same Church that has been most responsible for the transmission of the 'Gospel tradition' has also played the role of enforcer of 'law and order' against the oppressed by

divinely sanctioning the 'tradition of the State' from the fourth century on." For this reason, a Black articulation must "focus as much on the broader Christian tradition of the Black Church in America as it does on that of white, western Catholicism."[24]

In the clear and far-reaching vision of Dr. Eugene's remarks, she has convincingly named the liturgical imperatives that parallel and complement those for effective catechesis in the African American Catholic community. As in catechesis, African Americans bring their whole selves to worship, and therefore to the praise and thanksgiving of God within the framework of the Roman Church. They bring their cultural consciousness, their Black American history, their loyalties and relationships, their role models (both biblical and cultural), their longings and expectations, their achievements, and their failures. They bring their worldviews, customs, behavioral norms, affective modes, primary myths, expectations, values, philosophies, concerns, social location and circumstances, needs, and hopes. They also bring their understandings of the transcendent and the meaning of being human, holy, and humane. These are the constitutive dimensions of their individual and collective personhood that the African American Catholic community brings to ritual prayer. Nurturing this community's faith into maturity through a Black articulation of the Catholic Christian faith is therefore not only a requirement of effective catechesis, but also a demand of effective liturgy. The outcome of such a catechetical endeavor will ultimately benefit liturgical preparation and celebration by enhancing the formative potential and impact of liturgy and by helping to construct the theological foundations from which it emanates.

Father Edward K. Braxton: "Religion, Values, Ethnicity and the Black Experience"

Father Edward K. Braxton,[25] addressing the symposium on the interplay of religion, values, ethnicity, and the Black experience,[26] chose to offer "schematic reflections" on these topics, presenting several conceptual frameworks within which symposium participants might reflect on the complexity of human and cultural experience.[27] His formulations speak informatively and eloquently to Dr. Toinette Eugene's contention that catechesis and worship within the African American community are grounded in Black experience and Black theology. Moreover, his reflections are valuable to the work of constructing a holistic liturgical aesthetic—one that takes into account the full human experience of persons-in-community, in all their cultural-religious complexity, and that intends to foster the maturing relationship of these persons with God in faith, and therefore with questions of ultimate meaning.

Human Experience—Black Experience

Focusing first on Black experience, Braxton poses a critical question: What constitutes "the Black experience"? Who sets out the criteria for evaluating it?[28] Although there is rightly a sense of commonality among African Americans, born of a shared history, there are clearly preferred differences within the community, signaled by different ways of self-designation—Black, African American, people of color. Yet who decides what is the normatively Black experience? Braxton replies that to penetrate and interpret the Black experience fully requires diligence, consistency, collaboration, and sensitivity to the complexities that are involved.[29] It is precisely these complexities that Braxton chooses to delineate by offering a set of frameworks within which to explore human experience—and by implication Black experience—in all its multidimensionality.

Braxton's first schema considers the complexities of human value-formation in relation to concrete good. Values, he observes, "are relational phenomena."[30] They are constructed as persons relate to objects, goals, activities, or other persons, "experience them as meaningful, [and] ascribe special significance or value to them." The dynamic process of value-construction is neither abstract nor theoretical; rather, it is primarily affective. One is "impelled toward value" by feelings, moods, emotions, affects that recognize beauty, truth, justice, or love, and desire to participate in these goods. Hence, to attend fully to people's values—a critical aspect of their religions and liturgical sensibilities—we must observe the affective process by which they enter into relationship with instances of concrete good. Consequently, in our attention to constructing a liturgical aesthetic, we must honor the emotive matrix of people's lives, realizing how critical it is to the way they ascribe meaning to the many relationships of their religious and social lives. Moreover, we must attend to the concrete events, activities, persons, and objects that shape their experience, since it is in these encounters that feelings are formed and values are formulated.

Braxton identifies five types of human values—vital, social, cultural, personal, and religious—and describes how they interact with each other. *Vital values* "are primal."[31] They deal with the most basic requirements of our physical lives—food, shelter, clothing, exercise—and create the condition necessary for other values to develop. *Social values* deal with the interpersonal, communal, economic, political, institutional, and educational dimensions of life. They govern the "building of the social fabric of the community," and move persons to respond to the "urgent issues of the day." *Cultural values* provide a means through which people define, interpret, enrich, and give expression to their sense of human-being-in-the-world through music, art, poetry, artifacts and the many arts of living. They enable members of an ethnocultural community to "qualify, enhance, and nuance human society's expression, prolongation, and interpretation of itself."[32] They serve as an evaluative lens by which persons interpret and choose which cultural expressions of the larger society they will self-appropriate. *Personal values* are related to people's sense of "fulfillment, authenticity, interpersonal relationships, love, intimacy, and self-transcendence."[33]

Braxton underscores the particular relationship of personal values to social and cultural values. He points out:

> When we have social values and cultural values in an adequate harmony, it is more or less possible for individuals to pursue personal values in a radical sense. If one's vital, social, and cultural needs are being met, there is a richer context for personal values, such as fulfillment . . . and self-transcendence to be pursued. This is the case because the prior values provide a kind of foundation for the more elusive personal values.[34]

Hence, people are freer to explore new or unfamiliar meanings and values when their social and cultural values are honored. Radical self-transcendence is possible only when people's social and cultural needs have been attended to.

Finally, *religious values* refer to "the horizon of ultimate meaning."[35] They engage a person in a quest for the "radical meaning of human existence." They enable one to ask, "What is the broadest horizon within which I can interpret the things that are happening to me" within these other arenas—physical existence, social relationship, cultural expressions, and personal experiences of intimacy? Religious values enable persons to find meaning in the great religious symbols, events, rituals, and traditions mediated within the cultural context in which they find themselves. In other words, the pursuit of religious values is concretely situated within the sociopolitical and cultural matrix of people's lives.

This last insight is critical in shaping a worship aesthetic that will engage communities fully and holistically in the "labor of liturgy."[36] To attend only to their religious value-formation without acknowledgment of their social, political, and cultural milieu is to misunderstand the complexity of human experience. Braxton points this out: although his schema offers a "logical order" for the formation of values, experientially, values interact, and at times, are confused.

People sometimes seek religious meanings to fill the void they experience when other areas of valuing are unfulfilled. Or they may confuse cultural values with religious values, and "think that the cultural achievement of one or another ethnic or racial group in its religious values is, in fact, the very religion being expressed." An equally grave misuse of religious values is made when "those who wish to deprive people [of] their social, cultural, personal, and vital values are happy if religion [meets] human needs in such a way that [people] are content to leave the other values unfulfilled." This misuse of religion denies the fact that religious values do not supercede cultural values any more than self-transcendence disembodies a faith-filled person. Religious values enable persons to refine and ennoble their cultural values. The foundational matrix of people's religious values emanates out of the cultural values that make a people—in this instance Black people—"a people."

Having laid out these foundational understandings of values and value-formation, Braxton introduced a second schema. Underscoring again that the "concrete fact of being human is extremely complex,"[37] he focuses now on seven patterns of human experience through which persons approach questions of meaning—the biological, psychological, social, aesthetic, dramatic, mystical, and intellectual. Since each pattern moves a person toward questions of ultimate meaning, each is therefore related to the liturgical and catechetical processes by which persons grow toward maturity in the faith.

The first, *biological pattern* of experience, states Braxton, "refers to our concrete condition of being biological, physical beings . . . in all its unfolding forms—youth and vigor, peak years and maximum productivity, the autumn of life's declining, old age and death."[38] Bodily in character, the biological pattern of experience raises questions of meaning in the reflective person: "How and why am I this sort of being and what is the significance of this condition?" The question arises out of the particularity of one's humanness and seeks to give "radical meaning" to his or her actual physical condition.

The second pattern that Braxton identifies is *psychological* in nature—"the world of our interiority, the world of moods, feelings, affects, the world of changes in our interiority which cannot seemingly be explained by external circumstances."[39] Each person has within him / herself a "vast . . . internal communication system" that is most often unexplainable but nonetheless real. Through the impetus of "dispositional shifts"—changing inclinations, attitudes, or moods—this communication system enables persons to perceive, interpret, and weave the many experiences of life into a coherent network of meanings. Within this pattern, "the question of ultimate meaning can emerge," although the question, at this point, does not "necessarily mean an affirmation of the answer."

The *social pattern* of human experience, Braxton states, "is the pattern of our social intercourse," including "the world of intimacy, the world of being a friend, and being befriended; . . . of being in love and being a lover."[40] At the same time, this pattern "provides one with the disarming knowledge that one's soul's space has an existential void in it even when one has many friends." This "radical aloneness," this awareness that "the plentitude of one's soul-space is not adequately filled . . . .led an Augustine to say our hearts are restless until they rest in God."

A fourth, *aesthetic pattern* "is the encounter with tone, color, form, order, [and] beauty," perhaps in the experience of "a golden sunset, magnificent foliage, the sweep of snow after a storm, the translucence of ocean waves"; or in the encounter with the work of an artist—"a poem, a symphony, a painting, or a sculpture." The aesthetic pattern of experience "puts us in touch with a kind of fullness of reality," and thus, Braxton contended, "the world of aesthetics is very close to the world of religious intuitions."[41]

Although all the patterns Braxton described are pertinent to religious ritual, aesthetic patterns are critical to the Black Catholic "performative values" we will identify later in this chapter. Aesthetic patterns guide the kind of artifacts people create and collect, the kind of spatial arrangement they find inviting and hospitable, and the meanings they ascribe to color, texture, and form. They guide a people's preferences with regard to music, literature, dramatic perform-ance, graphic art, and oratory, including the imagery and modes of expressiveness they prefer. Moreover, because they enable persons to grasp "a kind of fullness of reality," an apprehension of the whole created universe "as it is meant to be," aesthetic patterns awaken persons to understandings of God's kingdom, God's *shalom*, God's justice for the world, as these are mediated in worship.

The *dramatic pattern* of human experience views the world, and one's life in it, as narrative and story.[42] Beginning with one's per-sonal story, Braxton notes, this pattern reaches out in successive waves to "the family, the neighborhood, . . . the larger community in its ethnic, racial, or its religious dimension." Here one finds "values associated with rituals, traditions, pageants, foods, linguistic expres-sions, and idiosyncrasies [that] enlarge and concretize the dramatic context" of one's identity—what it means to be "Creole from Louisi-ana, or to be Black from the inner-city of Chicago."

The critical feature of this dramatic pattern is that it engenders people's need to consciously connect their story, their self-under-standings, to the larger world. Beyond one's own ethnocultural com-munity, this pattern of human experience reaches out to embrace the whole world, the entire cosmos, enabling persons to situate their story in a larger narrative, be that biblical or cosmological. Indeed, people fully expect to find their personal story already contained within these larger stories, and to discover that personal meaning is already an integral part of what constitutes the meanings of these great narratives. Braxton added that insofar as humans are storytell-ers, they are consequently "story hearers"—potential "hearers" of the Word. "If there were to be a divine storyteller, we humans would be unique as hearers of that word."

A sixth, *mystical pattern* of experience involves those "occasional glimpses of the whole" that invite persons into a "silent knowing," or a state of "communion or intimacy with the 'other'"—that is, a "harmonious communion" that requires neither words nor images.⁴³ This experience of mystical communication happens to persons in varying degrees and modalities. Examples of this experience from within the African American tradition abound. Howard Thurman, for example, a twentieth-century Black Protestant preacher, teacher, and mystic, wrote: "God is with me. Always there is the persistent need for some deep inner assurance, some whisper in my heart, some stirring of the spirit within me—that renews, recreates and steadies. Then whatever betides of light or shadow, I can look out on life with quiet eyes."⁴⁴

Likewise, Father Cyprian Davis notes that African American spirituality is, at heart, "contemplative in terms of prayer, holistic in terms of asceticism, joyful in terms of spiritual atmosphere, and community-based in terms of spiritual values."⁴⁵ Echoing these same images, Sister Thea Bowman describes how pervasive the mystical encounter is within the spiritual lives of Black people:

> Black spirituality is contemplative. To contemplate the living word in the silence of the midnight hour. To contemplate the living word while you're washing your dishes at the sink. To contemplate that living word in the time of trouble and share that word, because Black spirituality is communal. Black spirituality is joyful in the time of trouble. Black spirituality is holistic.⁴⁶

Thurman, Davis, and Bowman corroborate Braxton's description of the mystical pattern as "intimacy with the 'other.'" They imply further that Black spirituality "predisposes" African American people to such experiences—in worship and in everyday living—and requires of them that they express these ecstatic moments in ways that invite other persons "to have the same self-authenticating experience."⁴⁷

The final pattern of human experience, the *intellectual pattern*, "relates to the world in a discursive manner."⁴⁸ Being more detached and analytic than the others just explored, Braxton comments, this pattern engages the person in "questions of ultimate intelligibility." Although unable to answer these questions completely, the intellectual pattern of human experience moves ahead with confidence, trusting that the questions are indeed answerable.

While Braxton's purpose in delineating these patterns of human experience is neither liturgical nor performative, he has constructed a schematic framework within which to view the intricacies of the human person who brings his or her whole self to ritual prayer. Moreover, he offers a detailed exposé of the complexity of human experience that needs to be addressed when one speaks of the "Black experience" as the essential starting point for a Black Catholic liturgical aesthetic. "We have a tendency," he notes to his colleagues, "to either confront the whole and never sort out certain elements of the complexity, or to latch on [to] one element of the complexity and consider that one element to be the whole."[49]

In addition, the pathways of human experience Braxton has explicated relate to the *processes of conversion* by which persons grow into mature faith.[50] Braxton describes conversion as a "transformation of horizon" due to the personal grasp of foundational values.[51] As with human experience, conversion is multidimensional. "*Religious conversion* is a personal transformation that allows one to affirm the radically gifted, meaningful and mysterious dimension of being human in the world." Yet religious conversion is but one modality of the transformation of one's horizon and values that evolves in the "life-long process of deeper and more holistic conversion." *Theistic conversion* moves one's religious sense toward the apprehension and articulation of such understandings as God, all-loving, personal, intelligent, caring." *Christian conversion* opens one toward encounter with Jesus, the Christ, and enables the paschal mystery to become real in a person's life. *Ecclesial conversion* turns one toward "community, the embrace of tradition, history," and an acceptance of the foundational values held within this ecclesial tradition. *Moral conversion* "is the struggle for self-consistency in one's public and private worlds. *Intellectual conversion* recognizes the "unity of truth." It acknowledges the historicity of the human race, the limits of language, and the permanence of mystery. Hence it is comfortable with the tension that comes from the complexity of knowing."

All of these modalities of conversion are integral to how liturgical rites and rituals invite and shape people's growing maturity in faith and to how the performative values of the liturgical aesthetic we are constructing honor the religious identity-formation *and* the sociocultural matrix of their human lives. If worship is to lead to the gradual transformation of persons' horizon of meaning, then the multiple modes of conversion and the complex pathways of human experience and value-formation must be considered.

Black Theology

Having explored the complexities of human experience, and by implication Black experience, Braxton turned to a second source of Black liturgy and catechesis as spelled out by Dr. Eugene—namely, Black theology. Braxton contends that there are three primary contexts for doing theology—the ecclesial tradition, the academy, and the sociocultural matrix.[52] Each has its own "mode of mediation," its own skills and competence, its own "community of theological discourse." Together, and through their unique lenses, they intend to mediate the meanings of human values, patterns of human experience, processes of conversion, and the formation of human horizons. By acknowledging these contexts and their differing modes of mediation, Braxton provided a ground on which those striving to articulate a Black theology could situate and validate their efforts.

The *ecclesial tradition*, as context for the work of theology, "seeks to preserve, interpret, and rearticulate the meaning of the central faith vision of reality of [its] specific tradition."[53] Its primary mode of mediation is dogmatic; its purpose is to identify and preserve the established core tenets of a faith tradition by identifying those "documents, doctrines, and office-holders [that] have a privileged or normative position in the community's self-understanding." In contrast, theology in the context of the *academy* employs a "critical mediation, and its radical commitment is not the authority of a particular tradition, but the methodologies that are prevalent" within the university. Within this critical mediation, devoutly held beliefs may be questioned, examined, and reinterpreted.

Third, theology rooted within a *sociocultural matrix*—in this case, Black theology and other liberation theologies[54]—employs an "existential mediation." It is "concerned with the relevance of the values affirmed in the religious tradition for the concrete sociocultural situation." Existential mediation is always selective, judging many "burning issues in the other two contexts as insignificant" if they fail to address the pressing concerns of a particular people. "The irreducible starting point" in this context, Braxton contends, is "the struggle to concretize transforming values and to challenge the conscience of [those] who seem indifferent." Here the concern is "personal, communal, and practiced. How does the Christian interpretation of reality contribute to the transformation of evil in a concrete political and social order?" From this matrix of existential mediation, Braxton noted, flow the "profound statements that . . . are being made [at this symposium] about Black Theology and the Black experience in the Black Church." These are rightly the work of existential mediation; indeed, they must be.

It is no surprise, Braxton commented, that "these three theological communities do not exist in serene harmony."[55] He invited his hearers to be among those few people who "can move with grace and ease through these several communities" and "carry on constructive conversations within them." While holding firm to the necessary matrix of Black life and faith experience, he called participants—and those concerned with constructing an appropriate liturgical aesthetic for African American Catholic communities—to be "genuinely concerned about dogmatic mediation in the Roman Catholic tradition," as well as sensitive to the unique problems and challenges posed by the critical mediation of academic theology.

In concluding his presentation, Braxton held out this challenge to his colleagues, and to us—to so "penetrate" the experience of African American religious culture that they might gift the Church with what he described as a "classic" expression of this faith tradition.[56] A "classic," he noted, "so profoundly penetrates the particular that it illuminates the universal . . . for any human being who has an attentive spirit" and who attends to "what the work of art discloses." It is precisely in its penetration of the specific and particular—in the work of this chapter, a uniquely *African American* liturgical aesthetic—that "human experience is experienced at greater depth."

Aesthetically, liturgically, and theologically, there could emerge reflections, expressions, and styles of the Black Catholic experience in a hybrid, in the profoundest sense of that term. Such a penetration and reinterpretation of the Black experience could well produce classic expressions that . . . penetrate the particular experience in such a way that it illuminates the universal with a telling urgency and enriches the larger Church community with a much needed vitality! While this is a very real possibility, it can be *lost by lack of diligence*, lack of consistency, lack of collaboration, and lack of sensitivity to the complexities that are involved. Each of us must play our own parts if we are to find telling ways to manifest that which is of perennial significance in Black Catholic Christianity. In doing so, we may play a broad and deep part in the shape of the Church to come.[57]

Father Glenn V. Jean-Marie: "Black Catholic Worship: Celebrating Roots and Wings"

We turn now to two addresses to the Black Catholic Theological Symposium that focus specifically on worship in the African

American community, the first given by Father Glenn V. Jean-Marie[58] and the second by Father Clarence R. J. Rivers. Each has a unique salience for the construction of a liturgical aesthetic, and, as we will see, each places distinctive emphasis on elements that contribute to our formulation of performative values.

Although Jean-Marie was still a young priest in 1978, the passion and insight he brought to liturgy was known and respected by the symposium organizers. Invited to address the need for guidelines for African American Catholic liturgical celebration, Jean-Marie first acknowledged the context of Black life and worship.[59] "[W]e are living in a society," he claimed, "that denies the beauty of Black Humanity. . . . [S]ociety has not affirmed that God in His Goodness and Kindness has created me Black in His Image. For society, Blackness is only an accident of my existence and has no relation to the essence of my personhood."[60] Jean-Marie not only reaffirmed Blackness as a legitimate self-identification, but he also cautioned his hearers not to forget the potent and potentially debilitating effects of living in a society that rarely, if ever, affirms anyone's Blackness. Yet for African American people, he reminded them, it has been "our faith and our Black humanity that have enabled us to deal with the contradictions of life. . . . For we know that we must live the challenge of our brother Jesus by affirming our Black Humanity: 'Let your light shine before [all].'" Indeed, as Black people have sung for generations, it is God who can "make a way out of no way."

Jean-Marie rooted his vision for Black Catholic theology and worship in the religious music of the traditional Black Church, interspersing images and phrases from these songs throughout his presentation. His passion was evident, and his attention to his own social immersion in the wider Black community apparent in the references he cited, placing Malcolm X, Lerone Bennet, and James Cone side-by-side with the authors of the *Constitution of the Sacred Liturgy*. These Black authors, he believed, were coparticipants in the effort to merge liturgy with life, to weave Blackness with Catholicism. He called the Church to examine its complicity with the racist practices that continue to permeate American society.[61] He shared his conviction that the primary problem facing the development of authentic expressions of African American worship is the preoccupation of Church authorities with defending established tradition, rather than actively seeking ways to ennoble and develop it in response to the God who is always doing something new.[62] And he professed his belief in a liberating God who quickens the hearts and comforts the souls of Catholic Christians who are consciously and unapologetically Black, and who work to realize their full potential as mature and faith-filled persons.[63]

Black theology, Jean-Marie contended, must take seriously the "suffering, struggling, humiliation, and oppression" that has marked the journey of Black Americans throughout their history.[64] Likewise, the celebration of the Lord's Supper in African American communities must "[celebrate] the reality of our liberation in Jesus Christ and [call] us to fellowship with Him." For if the Eucharist is to be a "truly meaningful celebration" that can "touch the hearts of people [and] call people to conversion, if the Eucharist is to nourish people [and] inspire them to growth, and if the Eucharist is a celebration of liberation, then it must be grounded in, rooted in, real experiences of life." Black worship "celebrates the reality that we are Black folks created in God's Image, knowing full well that we are always to praise God's Name."

Jean-Marie thus established his foundational premise: the primary task of a truly African American worship is to take the Black experience seriously, and to acknowledge, interpret, celebrate, and share the God-inspired "truths" that are to be found there.[65] More specifically, "liturgical expression should grow out of, and be suited to, the needs of [each] congregation" within the broad spectrum of African American experience. In all cases, it must go beyond "including a few Black symbols in the Liturgy." Rather, the whole liturgy must be transformed and transfused with the words, bodily expressions, and symbolic elements that express what is believed and lived.

[A]uthentic Black Catholic Worship flows out of the rich experience of our people and all the elements working together produce the experience of Jesus being present with His people as they are being transformed in glory and power and in Blackness in His name and by His power. . . . Authentic Black Catholic Worship involves the totality of words, bodily actions and things which symbolically express what is believed, so that the doing of it will actively contribute to God's presence becoming a reality.[66]

Jean-Marie grounded his claims for this transformation of Catholic worship with the Black cultural ethos in the Catholic tradition itself, beginning with St. Augustine's *City of God.* "The Church recruits her citizens from all nations," writes Augustine, "and in every language assembles her community of pilgrims on earth; she is not anxious about her diversities in customs, laws, institutions; she does not cut off or destroy any of them, but rather preserves and observes them. Even the differences in different nations she directs to the one common end of peace on earth."[67]

These striking words of Augustine are echoed, centuries later, by Pius XII: "The Church does not despise or reject the characteristic genius of various peoples [but] gladly welcomes them as a new and varied adornment of its own culture."[68] "You may *and you must* have an African Christianity," reiterated Paul VI decades later, addressing the churches of Africa. "Indeed you possess human values and forms of culture which can rise up to perfection such as to find in Christianity a true . . . fullness and prove to be capable of a richness of expression all its own and genuinely African."[69] In light of these understandings, which were recapitulated in the *Constitution on the Sacred Liturgy,*[70] Jean-Marie claimed that a truly African American worship in the Catholic Church is not only valid, but of its nature, it will be innovative and creative. It will

break new ground and take new initiative . . . always realizing that our Black Experience determines the character and nature of our Worship. For when the Catholic Faith springs forth from the souls of Black Folks, a new interpretation, a new form, and a new style of celebration emerges. It reflects the cultural, historical, social and religious background of transplanted Africans.[71]

While positing that Catholic liturgy must be imbued with Black culture without a distortion of the liturgy's own "internal logic," Jean-Marie likewise claimed that African American culture has an "internal logic" of its own that may challenge current assumptions about Catholic rites. The spiritual and temporal priorities that spring from Black experience must be juxtaposed with the pastoral priorities of Catholic rites. Catholic homiletics, with its tendency toward explaining religious concepts, must give way to the dialogical oratory of the traditional Black Church. The language of prayer and preaching must yield its propensity for simple and terse prose and be crafted with the linguistic metaphors that linger in the faith-filled imaginings of Black believers. An imposed ambience must give way to culturally resonant symbols that carry layers of meaning for Black Catholics.

The "internal logic" of African American culture, Jean-Marie claimed, is evident in the worship of the traditional Black churches.[72] In these settings, "worship has truly reflected the depth experience of our people." Worship in the Black Church "celebrates life." It "reflects an openness, a free-style, and a close relationship to life in which the sacred and secular come together to affirm God's wholeness."

Black worship . . . is a creative experience in which the people embrace the Kingdom of God. Because Black people know that it was God's grace, God's strength, that kept them keeping on when the going got tough, they were able to proclaim: Amazing grace! . . . Black people are filled with God's grace, God's love.

For God is a "rock in a weary land, a shelter in a mighty storm, and a stronghold in the day of trouble."[73]

Suggesting that worship in the traditional Black churches can provide a helpful starting point for reflection on the Catholic liturgy of African American communities, Jean-Marie identified the main elements that constitute Black worship: "praying, singing, preaching, shouting, conversion, and testifying, [all] working together to acknowledge and affirm the unity of life in the midst of seeming contradictions."[74] As these modalities of prayer inform the thrust of Catholic worship, he suggested, four critical elements must mark Black Catholic liturgy: "PRAYING, PROCLAIMING, PREACHING, and PRAISING." These four elements, expressed in the distinctive style and expressiveness of Black worship, "work together for the glory of God." They are rooted "in the experience of our people," and in working together, "they create a dialogue among the congregation and minister," indeed among all members who "share in the priesthood of Christ, . . . which in turn creates a happening; thus we have CHURCH." Through these modes of worship, communities access "the reality of revelation . . . by entering into it fully with the surrender of our whole person."

Each of the core modalities of prayer by which Black Christians have worshiped God for generations can release the power of Catholic worship. In *proclaiming* the scriptures, Jean-Marie posits, "we tell God's story in such a way that one not only hears the Word, but feels the Spirit."[75] Proclamation in African American communities "becomes a testimony," not only of the biblical author, but "of the person reading and the community as well . . . a personal testimony of the glory and power of God in the person's life." *Praising* through songs enables an African American assembly to enter fully "into the experience of God's love as manifested in the life of the people." Indeed, "they are not simply singing a song or dancing a dance, but are living an experience and at the same time expressing a point of view"—that "God is a God of Justice and Great Kindness;" and that the "God of Jesus is one with them fighting against everything that hinders them from becoming what He created them to be." *Preaching*, Jean-Marie contends, "is at the heart of Black Catholic worship." This claim he rooted in Catholic reflections on the liturgy as well as in Black experience. The people of God are "formed into one . . . by the Word of the Living God," by which "faith is aroused . . . and nourished in the hearts of the believers,"[76] stated Vatican II. While this is true for all Catholics, preaching takes on a special urgency in the Black Catholic community.

> If we search for the sustaining factor of Black people, we will discover preaching. For we are a people of the Word. We are by culture, by history, a preaching-oriented people. We come from a preaching tradition. Preaching sustained and nurtured us during days of slavery. Preaching gave us hope "in those days when hope unborn had died." Preaching enables us to keep on keeping on. Preaching enables us to be truly opened to receive the Eucharist, the bread of life. So one of the greatest gifts we, as Black People, can give the Church today is Preaching. For in authentic Black Preaching, the Spirit is renewed.[77]

Just as we are "called to truly tell God's story through preaching," continued Jean-Marie, "in the same spirit we are called to *pray* God's story through the Eucharistic Prayer."[78] It is here, in the newly composed eucharistic prayer that he presented to the symposium, that Jean-Marie demonstrated clearly how the lived faith of the larger Black community offers a mediating theology for African American Catholics.[79] His prayer "understands and responds aggressively to Black people's complex historical, cultural, social . . . and vital situation."[80] Weaving images, metaphors, and song refrains that spring from the "orature" of African American communities—an orature cultivated in the dynamic context of Black worship—Jean-Marie gave voice to a unique and moving expression of the great prayer of thanksgiving that is at the heart of Catholic worship. We have only to listen to a few excerpts to hear its distinctive phraseology and to sense its power for Black Catholic worship:

Father, all powerful and everliving God,
we do well always and everywhere to give you thanks
For you are indeed our God, our help in ages past, our hope for years
    to come;
you are our shelter in the stormy blast and our eternal home.[81] . . .
We thank you for Jesus, your Blessed Word,
a lamp unto our feet and a light along our pathway . . .
We thank you for that [Holy] Spirit that rides in our hearts,
for your Spirit has brought us a mighty long way.
Through many dangers, toils and snares we have already come.
It was your Spirit that brought us safe thus far and your Spirit will
    lead us on. . . .[82]

God our Captain who never lost a battle, you are indeed the Lord of
    power and
might. We praise you through your Son Jesus who comes in your
    holy name,
all the way from heaven down to this low ground of sorrow.
Yes, he is the word that brings liberation . . . the hand you stretch
    out to sinners . . .
Oh Lord, our heavenly Master,
your Son Jesus, our heart-fixer and mind-regulator, . . .
[enables us to] bring to you the gifts entrusted to us,
the Bread of life and the Cup of eternal liberation . . .
Fill us with the breath of his Spirit, and through the sharing of this
    sacred fellowship, may Jesus search our hearts
and if he finds anything not planted by your right hand . . .
we ask you to remove it by the brightness of his coming . . .

cast it into the sea of forgetfulness, where it will never rise up again
against this world, nor condemn us at the bar of judgment.

Father . . . may we continue to walk in your power
together with all your saints and martyrs, Leo the Great, Benedict the
    Moor,
Monica, Augustine, Martin de Porres, the Martyrs of Uganda, John
    Vianney,
Joseph, Martin Luther King, Jr., . . . Malcolm X,
and all your living saints who are daily dying, fighting for your
    truth. . . .

Go behind us as a protecting angel and be by our side as a
    safeguard . . .
and when we have done all assigned to our hands,
and this old world can afford us a home no longer,
may we look back and see a well-spent life,
as you gather people of every race, language, and way of life
to share in the one banquet with Jesus Christ
who is indeed the way to that new world where the fullness of your
    peace will be revealed . . .[83]

Jean-Marie had thus brought to life the Catholic tradition of eucharistic praise and thanksgiving in language that resonates deeply
with the prayer discourse of African Americans. Indeed Black Christians of many denominations could readily identify with the language of this prayer. Ecumenical in its theological scope, the prayer
stretches out into a deeper sense of unity with the larger sphere of
Black Christianity.

At the same time, Jean-Marie had woven elements of Black praying, proclaiming, preaching, and praising into a great symphony of
praise that he intends will not only release a community's memory

of Jesus, but will also incorporate them dynamically in Jesus' mission. To be drawn into the full power and potential of eucharistic praying is to be called to the transformative work of God. African American Catholic worship is "priestly, prophetic, *and* apostolic," Jean-Marie claimed. It affirms and judges, but it "also calls one to service."[84]

In celebrating the Eucharist we receive the grace and strength to do the same as Jesus: to be able to proclaim—as we celebrate God's love in worship—[that] His love is being enfleshed, is being made real. So, the celebration of the Lord's Supper is not to be viewed as an escape from the problems of life. But it enables us to deal with the contradictions of living on this low land of sorrow as we march on to Zion. It gives us the strength to be about the struggle of liberation. . . . Like Jesus, if we do not break our bodies and pour out our blood in loving service, . . . then we have nothing to celebrate, nothing to offer. Jesus was about serious business when He said: "Do this in memory of me." The words of the entire Eucharistic Prayer refers to us and gives us a [blueprint], a road map on how we are to live. . . . If we are not about the business of liberation, of service, our celebrations, no matter how well planned, beautiful or filled with Black symbols will be nothing . . . people will only be entertained. . . . "For the Son of Man . . . came not to be served, but to serve, and to give his life as a ransom for many" (Mk 10:45). This is what I believe authentic Black Worship is all about: being PRIESTLY, PROPHETIC, AND APOSTOLIC.[85]

The priorities and perceptions set out by Glenn Jean-Marie speak eloquently and informatively to our task of constructing a lexicon of performative values that embody a Black Catholic liturgical aesthetic. In sum, he underscores eight important values for worship within

African American communities: (1) that in taking the Black experience seriously, worship affirms the God-given dignity of Black humanity; (2) that liturgy celebrates liberation in Jesus Christ and the call to fellowship with him; (3) that, beyond including a few Black symbols, the whole liturgy must be transformed with the ethos and expressive modes of African American religious culture; (4) that African American Catholic liturgy will be innovative and creative, reflecting the cultural, historical, social, and religious background of the people; (5) that the "internal logic" of Catholic worship will need to be harmonized with the "internal logic" of traditional Black worship, which reflects an openness, a free style, and a close relationship with life; (6) that praying, proclaiming, preaching, and praising will be the core modalities of liturgical prayer, each releasing, in their distinctive expressiveness, the power of Catholic worship, and working together, create a dialogue among ministers and all participants who share the priesthood of Christ; (7) that the prayer language of Catholic worship will be transformed by the "orature" of the African American religious culture; and (8) that worship will both release the community's praise of God and incorporate them into the mission of Jesus.

In concluding his presentation, Jean-Marie underscored the importance of this work for future generations. There are "only two lasting bequests" that we can hope to leave future generations, he noted: "one of these is roots, and the other wings."[86] In "authentic Black Catholic Worship," African American communities celebrate both. "We celebrate our roots; roots of our humanity, roots of our faith, roots of our heritage. . . . [W]e proclaim to the world the joys of being created Black and that God is Good!" At the same time, "We know because of the Resurrection [that] Jesus didn't allow us to be shackled by the bonds of death, suffering, and oppression." In worship fully alive, "He gives us wings to fly, to grow, to develop, to be creative. The Spirit of God is breathed [once again] into our hearts."

Father Clarence R. J. Rivers:
"The State of the Liturgy in the Black Catholic Community"

In 1978, the work of Father Clarence Rivers[87] had already precipitated, or at least inspired, most of the Black Catholic scholars at the symposium. As a nationally known liturgist, musician, and scholarly voice, he was perhaps better known than his colleagues. They were aware that for most of his priestly life he had striven to bring the genius of African American religious culture to the forefront of Catholic pastoral efforts, working especially on the development of liturgical music. His very presence at the symposium evoked the full spectrum of his leadership and insightful writings.[88] While his presentation to the symposium reiterated some of the themes contained in these sources, and which we have explored at some length in Part Two of this volume, Rivers' perceptions come into new relief in light of the intellectual ferment of this gathering. Asked to address the "state of the liturgy in the Black Catholic Community," Rivers summarized the situation as "somewhere between where it started and where it ought to go."[89] To make clear the dimensions of that journey, Rivers began with a brief historical look at the formation of the cultural and religious marginalization of African Americans in society, in the Church, and in its worship. Although doctrinally and scripturally the Church is neither Black nor white, "Greek nor Jew, slave nor free" (Gal. 3:28), Roman Catholicism in the United States has been radically white. African American culture has been "considered inferior, second class at best, and inadmissable to tasteful worship." Yet, Rivers pointed out, although this negative perception of Black culture has permeated European and American perceptions for several centuries, "Europeans did not always think of Black African society and culture as inferior." Not only did the European explorers who first encountered sub-Sarahan Africa in the fifteenth century speak admirably of the civilization they found there, but the king of Portugal and the king of Kongo "addressed correspondence to each other as fraternal equals."[90] In time, however, "economic necessity" demanded another perception; for without a claim that Africans were uncivilized, that sub-Saharan Africa was barbaric and savage, European traders could not in conscience despoil and enslave Africans. "So began the European American myth of African inferiority," a myth that has indelibly shaped the legacy of negative self-perception that has permeated much of African American society. Oppressed African Americans began to "accept their oppressors' view of them," giving rise to self-hatred and a notion that "looking like white folks" was the ideal.

During the intervening centuries since that first European-African encounter in the fifteenth century, claimed Rivers, "the seeds of Black dignity and self-esteem remained planted in the souls of Black folk and were nurtured there by the refreshing waters of Black religion."[91] They were cultivated in the traditional Black churches that took their primary thrust from traditional African religion. Here "Black self-identity was maintained; [here] this seed sprouted, flourished, and blossomed into the Black pride renaissance of the sixties." It is only by confronting this history, contended Rivers, and acknowledging that "European American society consciously or unconsciously fabricated the myth of African subhumanity to justify its own in humanity," that we can understand and address the Church's negative stance toward Black culture. "To consider the problem of Black culture within the Catholic Church," or, more specifically within its worship, "as merely or even primarily a question of aesthetic preference is a failure to understand history."

Turning to the present, Father Rivers reflected briefly on his own leadership, and how his initial focus on liturgical music led him to the deeper implications of a truly Black Catholic liturgy. "The more I worked with music and worship, the more I began to perceive that within the Western mind there was a dichotomy between music and prayer."[92] Yet unless text and music are "made one within the person who was [composing] it, and one within the person who was to deliver it, it [will remain] void and without meaning."[93] Analogously, unless the entire worship event is constructed to the rhythms of Black life, people will not be transformed, individually and collectively, through the process of communal prayer. It is "not enough to introduce Black music into the liturgy," stated Rivers emphatically, echoing the words of Jean-Marie, "but [it is] necessary to bring the whole range of Black culture to bear on our worship."[94]

For many Black Catholics, Rivers contended, Catholic liturgy does not create meaningful channels for understanding their personal and religious lives. The social, political, affective, emotive, ideational, and physical aspects of their daily lives are too often split from the rituals of their Catholic identity. He attributed this disconnection between liturgy and life to a lack of balance, cohesiveness, and performative excellence in their worship. Hence, his goal became twofold: to find an "aesthetic cohesion" within the liturgy as a whole, based in a full and integral use of African American expressive culture and ethos, and to foster the artistic integrity and performative excellence of every aspect of the event. Since music was one of the first elements to reach some level of dynamism in many Black Roman Catholic communities, Rivers uses this as a touchstone:

> The lack of poetry either in active performance or in written composition [of prayers] has led to ineffectual proclamation of the word in the liturgy and to aesthetic incoherence in the Liturgy. Black music separated from Black prayer styles and Black preaching styles disjointed the Liturgy. And the presidential prayers of the Mass, especially the Eucharistic prayer, the readings, and the preaching paled, as it were, into insignificance alongside the

soul-touching music that was now being sung. The spoken prayers, the readings, and the preaching became dead spots, stopping
the dramatic movement, the flow of the service. And this imbal-
ance led misguided people to express the view that the music
should somehow be suppressed or held back in order to give the
other parts of the Mass a chance to be heard. . . . [But the] very
opposite is the case. The other parts of the Mass need to be
brought up to the relative level of excellence that we are beginning to achieve in our musical performance.[95]

The standard of great poetry became Rivers' yardstick. Unless
praying, preaching, praising, and proclamation take on the full
stretch of poetic utterance, he contended, they do not have the power
to transform people, individually and collectively. Unless preachers
are taught the skills required to engage fully in the "art of preaching," not even our best "theology of preaching" can make their words
effectual for a community at prayer.[96] Unless the liturgy as a whole
becomes a synchronized unit of thought, movement, text, and cultural expression, it will lack the poetic coherence to draw an assembly
into a fully embodied and heartfelt prayer. Any "separation of heart,
mind, and behavior on the part of liturgical ministers impedes the
effectiveness of worship."[97] Any "tendency to move and gesture without conscious deliberateness undermines the dynamism of the entire liturgical event." Lectors must be prepared to proclaim in such a
way that they "manifest the faith-filled conviction and urgency of a
people who must speak the sacred Word upon which they rest their
hearts." Only with attention to artistic integrity of each aspect of the
performative whole can the worship reach its full potential. Artistic
performance and performative competence, Rivers contended, are
ultimately and always at the service of spirituality. In striving for
excellence, we must "train our preachers, readers, prayers to become
fit instruments of the Holy Spirit," so that the liturgy as a whole

can become "an effective channel for the Spirit that leads [people] to ongoing *metanoia*."[98]

For Rivers' vision of excellence to be achieved—and the task remains urgent, he told symposium participants—all other disciplines must be put at the service of liturgy. We must "bring our collective imaginations," resources, and perspectives to address the challenge of vital worship, he stated. Without such efforts, all other theological, ethical, and pastoral efforts will be diminished and ineffectual.

> The chief job of any religious group is to help people reach beyond the here and now, beyond the status quo. Beyond the finite boundaries of this world, to reach the transcendent, to be in touch with God. If religion does all other things and fails in this one thing, it fails totally. All our work in education, charity, in seeking justice and civil rights and economic liberation and cultural freedom will wither and die. For indeed it is our ability to reach beyond the here and now that makes any human progress possible, even at what some people consider the merely humanistic level. Even at the merest humanistic level (and I don't believe there is such a thing) a sense of transcendence is necessary, otherwise people stagnate, stay where they are, and like stagnant waters are open to [decay]."[99]

It is precisely this call to enable persons to "reach the transcendent" that led Rivers to claim that worship must be their first and enduring priority. The danger is to simply "continue the conversation"—to address the challenge of creating a rich, authentic Black Catholic worship by seeking "a new rationale or a new theology which might . . . trigger change"[100]—when what is needed is a collaborative dedication to discovering a culturally resonant liturgical artistry. The task of articulating a Black Catholic theology is indeed critical; but if worship is not a priority, people will "stagnate spiritually and humanly." Moreover, it is in the liturgical arena itself, Rivers contended, that proper catechesis can be fully embodied. It is while consciously engaging in the liturgical enterprise that the deep psychic healing and assurance people are seeking can occur within Black individuals and communities. It is while actively participating in a liturgical event that the real and urgent demands of peoples' lives can seem manageable. The humanity of African American Catholics requires substance and drama, beauty and prophetic power if they are to transcend the troubles of this world.

"We must pool our resources," concludes Rivers, "improve and multiply the number of parishes where Black culture is welcome, and establish standards of excellence lest those who have already done so fall into mediocrity."[101] We must "develop and multiply through appropriate training" successors to those highly competent musical leaders that have already emerged. We must generate training programs that can nurture the skills of priests, deacons, and lay persons, so that their leadership of prayer will inspire their people, will "soften up our hearts of stone with the dew of the Spirit." We must discover ways to ground our creative efforts in the Roman rite, while using our own religious sensibilities and the ritually "sophisticated arts and skills" of the traditional Black Church, to enable Catholic worship to respond to African American religiosity, which demands emotional, dramatic, and soulful performance. In these efforts, we must continue to foster "cultural interchange between ourselves and our brothers and sisters in the Caribbean, Latin America, and, of course above all, in Mother Africa," engaging in a dialogue that can further stimulate our collective action.

Ultimately, it is within local worshiping communities, and on their behalf, that these efforts will come to fruition. Within local assemblies, Rivers stated, a striving for performative excellence is always "for the sake of the congregation,"[102] aimed at enticing and encouraging their full participation. Purposeful improvisation within the liturgy, guided by local liturgical leaders, should always be grounded in a knowledge of their people—"what makes people tick,

[and] how to make them tick."[103] The artistic movement and gesture of ministers, their exhibiting an "air of certainty" in all they do, should communicate that the assembly's own role as "prime witnesses of the faith" is respected. The overall impact of the worship must be to facilitate a Black community's legitimate pursuit of liberation in the here and now, while giving them a foretaste of victory to be enjoyed in the hereafter.[104]

Rivers and Jean-Marie: Two Strands in a Common Web?

In their symposium presentations and their broader liturgical leadership, Fathers Glenn Jean-Marie and Clarence Rivers place differing emphasis on what is most vital to Black Catholic worship. Although they agree on several basic premises, their divergent priorities cause us to ask, How do these viewpoints address the religious diversity of African American Catholic communities? And how do they inform the construction of a liturgical aesthetic?

Rivers, taking a more "classicist" approach to liturgical celebration, would not necessarily discard the well-made vesture, the gold and silver inlaid vessels, the pomp and sobriety of long processions, and the music (Bach, Handel, and Gregorian chant) that some would find unsuitable for Black worship. He would insist on scripted and well-rehearsed liturgical celebrations, with well-crafted gesture and a well-prepared congregation. Assembly participation would be expected, but Rivers would argue that "well-groomed" ministerial actions in the midst of the assembly are pivotal to the active engagement of the community, who need to be smoothly guided through the liturgical event. In Rivers' perception, these are the hallmarks of a celebration that is both Black and Catholic. Individual and collective transformation of the gathered assembly is fostered, he would argue, through the sheer beauty and grandeur of the event.

Jean-Marie, in contrast, would identify with and symbolically seat himself among the liturgical assembly. His would be a congregation expectant of transformation through the "free agency" of the Holy Spirit. This assembly would sometimes follow and sometimes direct the enactment of its liturgical celebration. Participants would turn readily to the "friend they have in Jesus" who sits beside and guides all their praiseworthy endeavors. Highly participatory and spiritually motivated, this assembly would anticipate an "indwelling" of the Spirit. They would welcome the Spirit's warm presence without restraint, and take whatever time is necessary to follow the promptings of this Spirit. This assembly would also trust itself to discern the appropriateness of its spontaneous but well-grounded ritual fluidity. The transformative potential of liturgy would be achieved by the palpable energy, passion, and spirit participants bring to the enactment of the liturgical event.[105] Attending to the prayer needs of the community would take precedence over rubrical adherence or preoccupation with normative liturgical practices because, Jean-Marie would argue, effective Black worship requires the community to "pray in the language, style, imagery, and spirit of [the] people." Worship necessarily "breaks new ground."

How can we harmonize these differing viewpoints? It is my conclusion that the philosophic and liturgical moorings of these two scholars are complementary rather than oppositional. With the foundation of a well-articulated catechetical base, both assemblies would have a strong sense that they are cocelebrants with their liturgical leaders and that their input is critically important to the liturgical enterprise. Yet the distinctiveness of Rivers' and Jean-Marie's visions underscores that a Black Catholic liturgical aesthetic must address the pluralistic ethno-religious continuum of the African American Catholic community. The merits of each liturgical vision is best understood if examined in light of the other, giving fuller definition one to the other. Both must and will be accounted for in the performative values to which we now move.

An African American Catholic Liturgical Aesthetic: Recapitulation and Distillation

It has become evident in the course of this chapter that the articulation of an African American liturgical aesthetic—that is, understandings of what is beautiful, sacred, praiseworthy, profoundly expressive, and life-giving for African American worshiping communities—must be rooted in an expansive vision of that community's history, culture, spirituality, and sociopolitical context. As the four scholars just explored make clear, such an aesthetic must be grounded in an affirmation of the dignity of Black humanity, and take as a starting point the African American experience in all its complexity. It must recognize the locus of God's revelation within African American life, while acknowledging, interpreting, and celebrating the God-inspired truths that are found in that lived context. It must respect the emotive matrix of people's lives, and honor their modes of value-formation and their search for ultimate meaning. It must realize the potency of Black symbols of faith, and embrace the distinctive modalities of prayer, preaching, singing, and praying that mark Black Christian worship. Moreover, it must offer the potential of a Catholic worship transformed by the wisdom of African American ethno-religious culture and theology.

Taken together, these four scholars have laid out multiple dimensions of a truly African American liturgical aesthetic, and have stressed the urgency of its realization in Catholic worship. It is our task now to distill their perspectives into a lexicon of "performative values"—to transpose their insights into a practice-oriented, practical recapitulation that can guide the work of African American communities, their leaders, and ministers into the future.

Before listing the twenty-three performative values I have identified, it is important to note that they are meant to coalesce in a common goal, one which has been eloquently expressed by Dr. Toinette

Eugene—to gather an entire African American community "in a participatory experience of deepening maturity in the faith," while "utilizing and leaning upon God's gracious Word and Presence . . . as revealed in the midst of Black struggle, survival, and success, so as to build up the believing community as persons who "collectively profess the Lordship of Jesus Christ, . . . accept the liberating presence of God's Holy Spirit," and embrace the call to participate prophetically in the mission of Jesus, the transformation of the Church's life, and renewal of all peoples.[106]

Lexicon of Performative Values

1. The whole range of African American culture is brought to bear on the liturgy: that is, Black experience, history, values, worldview, cosmology, dominant dispositions and self-understanding, preferred moods, ways of perceiving, methods of valuation, behavioral norms, spirituality and religiosity (including characteristic ways of defining and satisfying "soul space"), affective modes, ways of being a friend and being befriended, role models, primary myths and symbols, understandings of life, expectations, concerns, hopes, metaphors, images, aphorisms, proverbs, modes of expression (interactive and oratorical style), music, art, artifacts, and artistry (*Rivers, Eugene, Jean-Marie, Braxton*).

2. The Black experience is taken seriously, and the community seeks, first and foremost, to articulate, acknowledge, interpret, celebrate, further develop, encourage, and share the God-inspired "truths" it contains (*Rivers, Eugene, Jean-Marie, Braxton*).

3. Black culture, spirituality, and religiosity are broadly defined so that the range of resources brought to the liturgy is not arbitrarily constricted, nor the ethno-religiosity of the Black community stereotyped or caricatured, by the cultural or religious preferences

and biases of a few members of the community (*Rivers, Jean-Marie, Braxton*).

4. The wisdom, scholarship, and expertise of Black Catholic theologians and pastoral leaders are used as "sources" for developing a Black hermeneutic—one that extends beyond Roman Catholicism and the larger Christian community to include the wisdom, scholarship, and expertise of the pan-African community (*Rivers, Eugene, Jean-Marie, Braxton*).

5. This Black hermeneutic is consistently and comprehensively applied to scripture, doctrine, and the understandings of Christian discipleship that are operative in the liturgy (*Jean-Marie, Eugene*).

6. The constitutive elements, words, and actions of the liturgy foster the ongoing catechesis of liturgical ministers and the larger parish community—that is, an ever-deepening education and formation of the values and meanings they ascribe to their patterns of human experience—so that they may overcome any ignorance of, or negative attitudes toward, Blackness, a Black cultural consciousness, or the inherent worth of their African American ethno-religiosity (*Rivers, Eugene, Jean-Marie, Braxton*).

7. Revelation—God's self-disclosure in the midst of African American life—is stressed as an essential source for constructing a Black articulation and celebration of the faith (*Eugene, Jean-Marie*).

8. The liturgical artistry and skills of the traditional Black Church are readily utilized to fashion the varied components of a liturgical event—that is, it makes use of poetic and dialogical oratory; it incorporates a broad range of religious music (spirituals, hymns, anthems, gospel, metered music); it makes conscious appeals to

the emotions and feelings of the assembly; it engenders a sense of enjoyment and psychosocial satisfaction among the assembly; it displays interactive familiarity between ministers and the rest of the assembly; and it strives toward good drama (*Rivers, Jean-Marie*).

9. The substantive content of the liturgy—environment, commentaries, prayers, proclamations, sermon, movement and gesture, music, and songs—is selected, structurally arranged, and stylistically expressed to maximize its ability to engage and inform "the whole person": that is, each of the five types of human values and all seven patterns of human experience (*Braxton, Eugene, Jean-Marie, Rivers*).

10. The overall pastoral and catechetical priorities that guide the development of the liturgical event consciously and explicitly seek to foster transformation—a change for the better—within individuals and in their interpersonal relationships; among specific groups; within the larger parish community; and within the larger cultural, societal context (*Rivers, Eugene, Jean-Marie, Braxton*).

11. Conversion, forgiveness, and reconciliation are hallmarks of the worship—that is, the faults and failures found within the worshiping community, the Church, and the larger society are plainly acknowledged, and concrete ways for these persons, groups, and institutions to overcome their weakness are proposed (*Rivers, Eugene, Jean-Marie*).

12. The assembly is recognized as the "primary witnesses to the faith": that is, they are encouraged to affirm the beliefs, concerns, sentiments, and aspirations expressed in the liturgical prayers, proclamation, preaching, and music/songs through gesture,

movement, dance, handclapping, or verbal responses (*Rivers, Eugene, Jean-Marie, Braxton*).

13. The assembly is deliberately and consistently exhorted to express praise and gratitude to God in spite of the contrarieties and hardships they face as individuals and as a community (*Rivers, Eugene, Jean-Marie, Braxton*).

14. The structure of the liturgy is both coherent and fluid, allowing for a spontaneity that comes from the unexpected promptings of the Spirit, as evidenced in testimonies, requests for prayer, or ecstatic witness from members of the assembly (*Rivers, Jean-Marie*).

15. Balance and harmony among the individual parts of the liturgy are evident: each part has its own beauty and merit, but "blends" naturally with the other parts: for example, the music does not "carry the freight" of the Black experience, nor does the sermon alone bear the weight of the liturgy's formative / educative function (*Rivers, Eugene, Jean-Marie, Braxton*).

16. The physical and psychosocial environment, as well as the commentaries, prayer texts, proclamations, and music of the worship, must "work together"—that is, they are selected / created around a unifying focus or theme and are based in a Black hermeneutic (*Rivers, Eugene, Jean-Marie, Braxton*).

17. Preaching and prayers point to eminence of God; that is, they: (a) give witness to God's ongoing activity in the life of the community; (b) provide a faith-based commentary on the realities of Black life; (c) facilitate the assembly's ability to believe they can conquer and transcend life's hardships; (d) invoke the Spirit in

ways that inspire, uplift, comfort, instruct, and motivate the community to make their lives more whole and holy, and the world more human and humane; and (e) foster the community's ability to pursue liberation and salvation (*Rivers, Eugene, Jean-Marie, Braxton*).

18. Commentaries, prayers, proclamations, sermons are spoken as if their message is urgent and comes from the heart (*Rivers, Eugene, Jean-Marie*).

19. The "internal logic" of the Roman rite is attended to, recognizing that pastoral discernment may suggest that the structure of the rite may need to be modified—through rearranging the order of ritual elements or creating new ones—to suit the "internal logic" and pastoral needs of the local African American community (*Rivers, Jean-Marie*).

20. The Roman Catholic ritual tradition, with its Eurocentric predilections, is thus not denigrated or discarded, but rather adapted and used to suit the diverse spiritual and cultural preferences and prayer needs of the local community (*Rivers*).

21. The quality of the ritual performance gives evidence that the various liturgical ministers have the needed charism and competence for their respective ministries (*Rivers, Eugene, Jean-Marie*).

22. The preparation of all liturgical ministers fosters performative excellence, meaning that: (a) each minister's role is known and well-rehearsed, such that their posture, words, and actions seem "natural" and spontaneous; (b) they exude an "air of certainty"; and (c) they engender a sense of "trust" from the assembly (*Rivers, Eugene, Jean-Marie*).

23. The liturgical event is planned in collaboration with representatives of the varied liturgical ministers who participate in it (including presider, preacher, music director), as well as an informed group of persons from the larger parish community who can speak to the pastoral needs of the community (*Rivers*).

Conclusion

The performative values just outlined are, in many ways, a distillation of much that has been explored in this volume. Hence they provide both a fitting conclusion to the work and a bridge to the future.

It is our hope that for African American Catholic communities, these performative values, and the liturgical aesthetic they mediate, will facilitate an even deeper "penetration and reinterpretation" of Black religious culture. In so doing, Black Catholics will continue to gift the Church, as Edward Braxton proposes, with "classic" expressions of Catholic worship that can illuminate "the universal with a telling urgency and enrich the larger Church community with a much needed vitality."[107] At a time when Black Catholic leaders seek to reengage the struggle to forge culturally liberating expressions of Catholic worship for a new millennium, the insights distilled here can remind them of what should not be forgotten or misrepresented, and help to reignite the passion and energy of the decades explored in this volume.

For those beyond the African American Catholic community, these chapters hold out a model for the careful historical, theological, liturgical, social, and religious probing that can help a community of faith acknowledge its religious-cultural depths and express those understandings and predilections in worship. Moreover, they invite a deeper understanding of Black religious culture and liturgy. By focusing on worship practice, they reveal how the interplay of cultural consciousness, ritual resourcefulness, local agency, and charismatic leadership has enabled African American Catholics to claim their new and rightful place within the spectrum of the Church's catholicity, and to reclaim their full heritage as members of larger Black Christian Church in the United States. At a time when the cultural complexity of American Catholicism is on the increase, the struggle and wisdom of Black Catholics documented in this volume can stimulate new insight and invite new intercultural dialogue, while holding out a torch to leaders of other cultural communities to "let their own light shine!"

Clarence R. J. Rivers, 1931–2004

F ather Rivers' books *The Spirit in Worship* and *Soulfull Worship* challenged and inspired parishioners and pastoral liturgists alike to examine Catholic worship through the lens of African American soul. Never before had there been such a serious consideration of the value of the spirituality of this particular and peculiar people. "Black and Catholic" in the larger Black community was considered an anomaly; in the broader Catholic academic halls of learning such a consideration was a curiosity at best.

Clarence Rivers wrote the seminal text for African American Catholic liturgical rites and rituals. Though it was not his express intention to herald Black liturgy, his work emanated from such a deeply spiritual and historical perspective that his personal, spiritual essence poured forth and vested liturgy in her proper universal dress, the gown of Blackness.

Clarence Rivers knew that everyone was fashioned of the same clay and enlivened with the same spirit. His greeting to most was "Your Grace!" because all are, in the words of scripture, "Heirs of God and co-heirs with the Christ." His was not a useless, impotent symbolic language, but a language filled with life, which had to be enacted with corresponding respect. All human talent and skill should be relentlessly pursued, implored, and employed, he believed, for the sole purpose of glorifying God. His observations on Catholic Church life were firmly awash in baptismal responsibility and a practical theology.

With one foot in Africa and the other in the New World, he felt that African Americans, by virtue of their historical journey in the United States, had perspectives of which few others were capable.

He urged Church leaders, especially those who were Black, to "accomplish much, not by being pushy, but by simply speaking up as the Spirit prompts, on behalf of righteousness, on behalf of the disenfranchised, and on behalf of the still to be finished kingdom of God." His was to use "all of scripture, philosophy, theology and poetry" for the express purpose of glorifying the God who made us. As he wrote in a letter to a prominent African American Church authority, the employ of the intellectual attributes found in his store would bring forth the "mantel of leadership to drape itself gently, without effort or fanfare, around his shoulders." He continually counseled those in leadership positions to "marshal their spiritual, educational, and aesthetic resources to do good for the whole church."

Clarence Rivers was a realist when he considered worship. "The worship of God is for human beings, not for God!" was his active premise. In his book *Reflections* he warns against liturgical fetishes or the objectification of anything that might impede the spiritual quest. He questioned the seeming elevation of impractical liturgical theologies in the Church's search for adequate liturgical expression. In parabolic character he writes:

During the era of passive participation that was a "silent prayer" fetish. Somehow, lack-of-sound became the equivalent of deep devotion and reverence. Now in the era of active participation, we sometimes make the decibels produced the sole measure of our "joy in the Lord." Neither position, of course, is absolutely right nor absolutely wrong. The moment of silent prayer is often enhanced if the meditation period is preceded by a rousing song. Instrumental music in the background can be a powerful aid to the imagination. On the other hand, experience tells us that to be always hearing noises (even intelligible ones) is soon to be hearing nothing (*Reflections,* 62).

In his later years, the pursuit of the discipline of astronomy captured his attention. As he learned more about the universe, he said, the more awesome God became. Ever relying on his early seminary education and its philosophical intellectual tradition, Clarence recalled Thomas Aquinas' adage that as our understanding of the cosmos expands, so does our view of God and our appreciation of the meaning and significance of the Gospel. In a galaxy of some one hundred billion stars, and a universe of some two hundred billion or more galaxies, all of nature bespoke the awesomeness of God.

—Ronald D. Harbor, 2006

I am seeking for a City, Halleluia!!!
For a City in that Kingdom, Halleluia!
And I don't feel no ways tired!
Oh, Glory Halleluia!

Deus in adjutorium meum intende!
Domine ad adjuvandum me Festina!
Festina!

Enlighten Us All!
For where there is no light, no prophetic vision
Surely people will perish!

—Clarence R. J. Rivers

Introduction

1. See David D. Hall, "Introduction," in *Lived Religion in America: Toward a History of Practice*, ed. David D. Hall (Princeton: Princeton University Press, 1997), vii–xiii. See also David M. Hammond, ed., *Theology and Lived Christianity* (Mystic, Conn.: Twenty-Third Publications, 2000), and Dorothy C. Bass, ed., *Practicing Our Faith* (San Francisco: Jossey-Bass, 1997).

2. See Craig Dykstra and Dorothy C. Bass, "The Theological Understandings of Christian Practices," in *Practicing Theology: Beliefs and Practices in Christian Life*, eds., Miroslav Volf and Dorothy C. Bass (Grand Rapids, Mich.: Eerdmans Publishing Company, 2002), 18.

3. See Hall, *Lived Religion*, xii. Sherry B. Ortner refers to practice as "culture in motion." See "Theory in Anthropology since the Sixties," *Comparative Studies in Society and History* 26 (1984): 126–166; as quoted in Hall, xi.

4. See Robert J. Schreiter, *The New Catholicity: Theology between the Global and the Local* (Maryknoll, N.Y.: Orbis Books, 2004), 75–78. Peter Phan explores a related concept of multiple cultural-religious belonging that applies equally well to African American Catholics. See his *Being Religious Interreligiously: Asian Perspectives on Interfaith Dialogue* (Maryknoll, N.Y.: Orbis Books, 2004), 67–78. Here he is talking specifically about the Asian multifaith experience, whereas in *Christianity with an Asian Face: Asian*

American Theology in the Making (Maryknoll, N.Y.: Orbis Books, 2003), 11–12, he refers directly to the African American experience. In a similar vein, Virgilio Elizando speaks of *mestizaje* to refer to the mixing of cultures fundament to Hispanic hybrid identity. See his *The Future is Mestizo: Life Where Cultures Meet* (Oak Park, Ill.: Meyer-Stone Books, 1988).

5. W. E. B. Du Bois, *The Souls of Black Folk* (Chicago: A. C. McClurg, 1903), 45–47.

6. See Schreiter, *The New Catholicity*, 77–78, for discussion of boundaries and their role in identity-formation within hybrid cultures.

7. Robert Schreiter notes that "with the advance in knowledge of plant genetics by the end of the nineteenth century, hybrids could be seen as not just different, but potentially superior to unmixed varieties." But, he comments, "such knowledge had a hard time penetrating the prevailing racialist and cultural discourse" that favored cultural and racial "purity." *New Catholicity*, 75.

8. See, for example, Mark Searle and David Leege, *The Notre Dame Study of Catholic Parish Life* (Notre Dame: University of Notre Dame Press, 1985), and *Liturgical Renewal, 1963–1988: A Study of English Speaking Parishes in the United States* (Washington, D.C.: Georgetown Center for Liturgy, Spirituality and the Arts, 1988). Although the latter study included a few parishes of other cultural backgrounds, the differences of experience were not foregrounded in the study's outcome.

9. I am grateful to Peter Phan for making this connection between liberation and inculturation in reference to Asian American Catholics. See *Christianity with an Asian Face: Asian American Theology in the Making* (Maryknoll, N.Y.: Orbis Books, 2003), xv.

10. David Hall speaks of the "politics of religious practice"—"on the one hand a 'politics of regulation' from the center, often with some measure of success; on the other an extraordinary array of practices arising out of custom, improvisation, and resistance." See *Lived Religion*, viii.

11. Agency is nothing new within the Black Christian experience. Albert J. Raboteau, in his *Slave Religion: The "Invisible Institution" in the Antebellum South*, states that "slaves did not simply become Christians; they creatively fashioned a Christian tradition to fit their own peculiar experience of enslavement in America" (Oxford: Oxford University Press, 1978), 209.

12. The 2006 Joint Conference of the National Black Catholic Clergy Caucus, the National Black Catholic Sisters' Conference, the National Black Catholic Deacons and their Wives, and the National Black Catholic Seminarians Association voted to initiate a national convocation to further the development of Black Catholic worship. See Joint Conference Proceedings, August 2006.

PART ONE   An Historical Overview:
The Emergence of African American Catholic Worship

1. Cyprian Davis, *The History of Black Catholics in the United States* (New York: Crossroad, 1990).

2. Cyprian Davis, "Evangelization and Culture in the Historical Context of Black America," in *Our Roots and Gifts* (Washington, D.C.: Archdiocese of Washington, 1989), 109–114. See also Davis, *History of Black Catholics.*

3. M. Shawn Copeland, "African American Catholics and Black Theology: An Interpretation," in *Black Theology: A Documentary History, Vol. II: 1980–1992,* ed. James H. Cone and Gayraud S. Wilmore (Maryknoll, N.Y.: Orbis, 1993), 99.

4. Ibid., 99. The First Black Catholic Lay Congress was held in Washington, D.C., in 1889. Other congresses include: 1890, Cincinnati; 1892, Philadelphia; 1893, Chicago; 1894, Baltimore.

5. Glenn V. Jean-Marie, "Black Catholic Worship: Celebrating Roots and Wings," in *Theology: A Portrait in Black,* ed. Thaddeus Posey, O.F.M. Cap. (Pittsburgh: Capuchin Press, 1980), 80.

6. Cyprian L. Rowe, "The Case for a Distinctive Black Culture," in *This Far by Faith: American Black Worship and Its African Roots,* ed. National Office for Black Catholics (Washington, D.C.: Liturgical Conference, 1977), 27.

7. See D. R. Whitt, "*Varietates Legitimae* and the African-American Liturgical Tradition," *Worship* 71, no. 6 (1997): 504–537.

8. See Melva Wilson Costen, *African American Christian Worship,* Second edition, (Nashville: Abingdon Press, 2007).

9. William B. McClain, "The Black Religious Experience in the United States," in *This Far By Faith: American Black Worship and Its African Roots,* ed. National Office for Black Catholics (Washington, D.C.: Liturgical Conference, 1977), 37.

10. Wilton D. Gregory, "Black Catholic Liturgy: What Do You Say It Is?" *U.S. Catholic Historian* 7, nos. 2 and 3 (1988): 317.

11. See Ronald L. Sharpes, "Black Catholic Gifts of Faith," *U.S. Catholic Historian* 15, no.4 (1997): 35–41. For the significance of the term "patrimony," see Whitt, "*Varietates Legitimae.*"

12. *Kairos*: as used by Paul in the New Testament refers to a "decisive moment," "a time rich in opportunity," or "eschatologically filled time." See Horst Balz and Gerhard Schneider, eds., *Exegetical Dictionary of the New Testament* (Grand Rapids: William B. Eerdmans, 1981), 232–233.

13. Copeland, "African American Catholics," 101.

14. Edward K. Braxton, "We, Too, Sing America" in *Our Roots and Gifts* (Washington, D.C.: Archdiocese of Washington, 1989), 91. See also Sharpes, "Black Catholic Gifts," 37.

15. In response to their demands, the U.S. Catholic bishops issued a "Statement on Race" (1968), but neither this document, nor its predecessor, "Discrimination and the Christian Conscience" (1958), fully redressed the persistent inequality experienced by African American Catholics.

16. The formation of the NBCCC was followed almost immediately by the organization of the National Black Sisters' Conference.

17. Vatican Council II, *Pastoral Constitution on the Church in the Modern World* (Washington, D.C.: USCC Publishing Office, 1965) nos. 53–62; Vatican Council II, *Constitution on the Sacred Liturgy*, in *The Liturgy Documents*, 4th ed. (Chicago: Liturgy Training Publications, 2004), no. 37.

18. *Constitution on the Sacred Liturgy*, nos. 37–38, 40. Subsequent conciliar and postconciliar documents restate and develop these principles. However, as we shall see later in this chapter, the Congregation for Divine Worship and the Discipline of the Sacraments issued a document entitled *Varietates legitimae (Inculturation and the Roman Liturgy)* in 1994 that would reinterpret the extent to which "legitimate variations" and "radical adaptations" can be made.

19. Address given in Kampala, July 31, 1969; quoted in Black Catholic Bishops of the United States, *What We Have Seen and Heard: A Pastoral Letter on Evangelization from the Black Bishops of the United States* (Cincinnati: St. Anthony Messenger, 1984), 3.

20. Pope John Paul II, "The Pope's Address to Black Catholics, " New Orleans, La., September 12, 1987. See also *Origins* September 24, 1987, 252.

21. Copeland, "African American Catholics," 103; Clarence R. J. Rivers, "'Thank God We Ain't What We Was': The State of the Liturgy in the Black Catholic Community," in *Theology: A Portrait in Black*, ed. Thaddeus Posey, O.F.M. Cap. (Pittsburgh: Capuchin Press, 1980), 68–70. See also Sharpes, "Black Catholic Gifts."

22. Sharpes, "Black Catholic Gifts," 49–50.

23. Copeland, "African American Catholics," 103.

24. Clarence R. J. Rivers, *Soulfull Worship* (Washington, D.C.: National Office for Black Catholics, 1974), 14.

25. Sharpes, "Black Catholic Gifts," 49.

26. Rivers, *The Spirit in Worship* (Cincinnati: Stimuli, 1978). See also Rivers, "Music and the Liberation of Black Catholics," *Freeing the Spirit* 1, no. 1 (1971): 26–28.

27. The NOBC, with the endorsement of the Bishops' Conference of the United States, functioned as an umbrella organization to focus attempts to make the Church relevant to the needs of the Black community.

28. Joseph Lawson Howze; Eugene Antonio Marino, S.S.J; Joseph Francis, S.V.D.; James Patterson Lyke, O.F.M., were ordained auxiliary bishops of Natchez-Jackson, Miss., Washington, D.C., Newark, N.J., and Cleveland, Ohio, respectively. Howze was named Bishop of Biloxi, Miss., in 1977, becoming the first Black ordinary in the United States since 1900.

29. See Sharpes, "Black Catholic Gifts."

30. Copeland, "African American Catholics," 104.

31. Rivers, "Music and the Liberation of Black Catholics," 28.

32. Leon C. Roberts, "The Development of African American Liturgical Music Since Vatican II," in *Our Roots and Gifts* (Washington, D.C.: Archdiocese of Washington, 1989), 30.

33. Copeland, "African American Catholics," 103.

34. Copeland, "African American Catholics," 105–106. Copeland cites a pastoral training program begun in Detroit in the late '60s to provide Black men with the theological, spiritual, and personal formation necessary to function in the Black community as lay or nonordained ministers.

35. Roberts, "Development of African American Liturgical Music," 29; Jacqueline C. Dje Dje, "An Expression of Black Identity: The Use of Gospel Music in a Los Angeles Catholic Church," *Western Journal of Black Studies* 7, no. 3 (1983): 153.

36. Celestine Cepress, *Sister Thea Bowman, Shooting Star: Selected Writings and Speeches* (Winona, Minn.: St. Mary's Press, Christian Brothers Publications, 1985), 59–60.

37. National Conference of Catholic Bishops, Secretariat for Black Catholics, and Secretariat for the Liturgy, *Plenty Good Room: The Spirit and Truth of African American Catholic Worship* (Washington, D.C.: USCC Publishing Office, 1990), nos. 61–62; Cepress, *Sister Thea Bowman*, 64; Wyatt Tee Walker, *The Soul of Black Worship* (New York: Martin Luther King Fellows Press, 1984), 56; Walker, *"Somebody's Calling My Name": Black Sacred Music and Social Change* (Valley Forge, Pa.: Judson Press, 1979), 52–54.

38. Joseph A. Brown, "Theological Themes within African American Religious Experience"; paper presented at the Conference on the Experience of African American Catholics in the Life of the Church, Annual Meeting of the African American Jesuits of the United States, Jesuit School of Theology, Berkeley, Calif., October 13, 1995. He highlights this "mystical identification" as an important theological theme within African American religious experience.

39. Costen, *African American Christian Worship*, 83–84.

40. Ibid., 83–85.

41. Dje Dje, "An Expression of Black Identity," 153.

42. Ibid. See also Dje Dje, "Change and Differentiation: The Adoption of Black American Music in the Catholic Church," *Ethnomusicology* 30, no. 2 (1986): 223–252; Mellonee Burnim, "The Black Gospel Music Tradition: A Complex of Ideology, Aesthetic, and Behavior," in *More Than Dancing*, ed. Irene V. Jackson (Westport, Conn.: Greenwood Press, 1985), 149; Walker, "*Somebody's Calling My Name*," 127–59.

43. Dje Dje, "An Expression of Black Identity," 153.

44. See Walker, "*Somebody's Calling My Name*."

45. Rivers, *Soulfull Worship*, 42.

46. Rivers, *The Spirit in Worship*, 15–48.

47. See, for example, Albert J. Raboteau, *Slave Religion* (New York: Oxford University Press, 1978).

48. Rowe, "The Case for a Distinctive Black Culture," 20–27.

49. Ibid., 23.

50. McClain, "Black Religious Experience," 29–37. What follows is summarized from this source.

51. James P. Lyke, "Application of Black Cultural Considerations to Catholic Worship," in *This Far By Faith: American Black Worship and Its African Roots*, ed. National Office for Black Catholics (Washington, D.C.: Liturgical Conference, 1977), 50–57.

52. Ibid., 57.

53. Ibid., 54–57.

54. Rivers, "'Thank God We Ain't What We Was,'" 70.

55. Jean-Marie, "Black Catholic Worship," 85.

56. Rivers, "'Thank God We Ain't What We Was,'" 73.

57. Ibid., 68.

58. Sharpes, "Black Catholic Gifts," 29.

59. Ibid., 29, quoting the *Buffalo Magnificat*.

60. Ibid., 30, quoting the *Michigan Catholic*.

61. National Conference of Catholic Bishops, *Brothers and Sisters to Us All: U.S. Bishops' Pastoral Letter on Racism in Our Day* (Washington, D.C.: USCC Publishing Office, 1979), nos. 1, 14. Ironically, the title indicates the centrality of white membership to Catholic life.

62. Black Catholic Bishops of the United States, *What We Have Seen and Heard: A Pastoral Letter on Evangelization from the Black Bishops of the United States* (Cincinnati: St. Anthony Messenger Press, 1984), 31.

63. The new bishops were Emerson Moore (auxiliary of New York, N.Y.); Moses Bosco Anderson, S.S.E. (auxiliary of Detroit, Mich.); Wilton Daniel Gregory (auxiliary of Chicago, Ill.); James Terry Steib, S.V.D (auxiliary of St. Louis, Mo.); John Houston Ricard, S.S.J. (auxiliary of Baltimore, Md.); Carl A. Fisher, S.S.J. (auxiliary of Los Angeles, Calif.): Curtis J. Gillory, S.V.D. (auxiliary of Galveston-Houston, Tex.); Leonard Olivier, S.V.D. (auxiliary of Washington, D.C.).

64. Black Catholic Bishops of the United States, *What We Have Seen and Heard*, 32; what follows is taken from this source, 8, 30–32.

65. *Sacrosanctum Concilium / Constitution on the Sacred Liturgy*, no. 37.

66. The vision of worship elucidated in this document lacks the breath of scope articulated by Clarence Rivers a decade earlier. Nor does it explicitly elaborate how the Black religious heritage might "overwhelm" the liturgy, or what is perceived as "a balanced unified action."

67. Black Catholic Bishops of the United States, *What We Have Seen and Heard*, 30.

68. Ibid., 32.

69. James P. Lyke, "Liturgical Expression in the Black Community," *Worship* 57, no. 1 (1983): 14–33. What follows summarizes key aspects of this survey.

70. *Fire in the Pews,* Oblate Media and Communication Corporation. A subsequent edition of the film was edited to eliminate scenes of George Stallings after his formation of Imani Temple.

71. The parishes were St. Augustine's in Washington, D.C.; St. Francis de Sales, St. Monica's, and Xavier University in New Orleans, La.; St. Teresa's and Holy Guardian Angels in St. Louis, Mo.; St. Mark's and St. Aloysius in Harlem, N.Y.; Holy Child Jesus, Caton, Miss.; St. Sabina, Chicago, Ill; Our Lady of Charity, Brooklyn, N.Y.; and Sacred Heart, Queens, N.Y. The most extensive coverage is given to St. Augustine's parish in Washington, D.C.

72. George Stallings was then the director of the newly established Office of Evangelization for the Archdiocese of Washington, D.C. The insights he brought to this documentary reiterate a liturgical theology that Clarence Rivers articulated in the 1970s and 1980s and situated Stallings at the heart of Black Catholic leadership in the 1980s.

73. Thea Bowman, in *Fire in the Pews.*

74. Ibid.

75. George Stallings, in *Fire in the Pews.*

76. Ibid.

77. Ronald L. Sharpes, "Black Catholics in the United States: A Historical Chronology," *U.S. Catholic Historian* 12, no. 1 (1994): 138. It is important to note that Black Catholic leaders originally decided not to place the NOBC under the auspices of the NCCB. In the 1980s, they reversed this decision to establish definitive ties with the Bishops' Conference, believing that fuller recognition was now possible and that Black bishops could expand the boundaries of episcopal decision makers.

78. Sharpes, "Black Catholic Gifts," 53. The Secretariat for Black Catholics was renamed the Secretariat for African American Catholics in 1991.

79. Copeland, "African American Catholics," 112.

80. National Conference of Catholic Bishops, Secretariat for the Liturgy, and Black Liturgy Subcommittee, *In Spirit and Truth: Black Catholic Reflections on the Order of Mass* (Washington, D.C.: USCC Publishing Office,

1987). An earlier form of this document, prepared by Black leaders, called for more self-determination and ongoing experimentation. However, this was rejected because it was perceived by the drafters of *In Spirit and Truth* that the time of post–Vatican II experimentation had ended.

81. Ibid., 2.

82. Ibid., 28; italics ours.

83. *Plenty Good Room*, nos. 123, 124.

84. Numerous persons were engaged in this process including representatives of various Black Catholic Organizations. See preface to *Lead Me, Guide Me* (Chicago: GIA Publications, Inc., 1987), 1.

85. Copeland, "African American Catholics," 105. A differing perception of the editorial process is offered by some on the editorial board who felt that decisions about what songs to include did not totally reflect the choice of the hymnal's Black editors.

86. Copeland, "African American Catholics," 105–107. What follows, including quotes, draws on this source.

87. The proposal was initiated by Father Al McKnight, C.P.P.S., a member of the NBCCC. The congress trustees excluded the proposal from the agenda on the grounds that the issue had not been raised within the [arch]diocesan reflection days, which identified the major topics for consideration by the congress delegates. Consequently, the only way to get the proposal on the agenda was to have fifty-percent-plus-one of the delegates sign a petition requesting that it be raised from the floor. This required that the petition be circulated, signed, and submitted to the trustees within twenty-four hours. Supporters of the initiative deemed the task to be impossible and abandoned the effort.

88. Pope John Paul II, "The Pope's Address to Black Catholics," 252.

89. See Giles Conwill, "The Word Becomes Black Flesh," in *Evangelizing Blacks*, ed. Glenn C. Smith (New York: Paulist Press, 1988), 58.

90. Ibid.

91. Bowman, "To Be Black and Catholic," *Origins* 19, no. 8 (July 1989): 115; italics ours.

92. Sharpes, "Black Catholic Gifts," 30–31.

93. D. R. Whitt, "Not Rite Now: An African-American Church?" *Church* (Spring 1990): 5–10.

94. Ibid.

95. National Black Sisters' Conference (NBSC) Joint Conference Minutes, 1989. Stallings expressed his hope that Imani Temple would receive "de facto" approval from the U.S. National Conference of Catholic Bishops, and Bishops Terry Steib and Wilton Gregory volunteered to be episcopal advisors to the venture.

96. The national organizations endorsed the need and hope for Imani Temple to have full episcopal approbation for ministerial experimentation. Stallings' break from the Roman rite was the result of his renunciation of some essential Roman doctrines in 1990. No Black Catholic organization has supported Stallings' departure from orthodoxy.

97. NBSC Joint Conference Minutes, 1989.

98. See Whitt, "Not Rite Now"; even though this article was not published until 1990, it is reviewed here because it aptly captures the sentiments of those who opposed the proposal.

99. Braxton, "We, Too, Sing America," 98–100.

100. Cyprian Rowe recently returned to the Roman Catholic Church.

101. The following images are drawn from *Plenty Good Room*, nos. 47–49, 85.

102. *Plenty Good Room*, no. 49.

103. Leopold Sedar Senghor, as quoted in *Plenty Good Room*, no. 85.

104. Images in this section are taken from *Plenty Good Room*, nos. 89–99, 102.

105. *Plenty Good Room*, no. 123.

106. Ibid., nos. 110–122.

107. See Mark Francis, "Liturgical Adaptation," in *The New Dictionary of Sacramental Worship*, ed. Peter E. Fink (Collegeville, Minn.: Liturgical Press, 1990), 14.

108. See Anscar Chupungco, "A Definition of Liturgical Inculturation," *Ecclesia Orans* 5 (1985): 13; Aylward Shorter, *Toward a Theology of Inculturation* (Maryknoll, N.Y.: Orbis, 1988), 191–194.

109. Ary Roest Crollius, "What Is So New about Inculturation?" *Gregorianum* 59, no.4 (1978): 733. See also Pope John Paul II, *Catechesis in Our Time (Catechesi Tradendae)* (Washington, D.C.: USCC Publishing Office, 1979), no. 53. John Paul II instructs catechists both to steep their learners in

the faith tradition and to call forth "original expressions of Christian life, celebration and thought."

110. Black Catholic Bishops of the United States, *What We Have Seen and Heard*, 17.

111. *Plenty Good Room*, v.

112. National Black Catholic Clergy Caucus, *Right Rites* (Opelousas, La.: African-American Catholic Rite Committee of the National Black Catholic Clergy Caucus, 1991).

113. Leonard G. Scott, "Canonical Reflections on the Study Conducted by the National Black Catholic Congress Regarding the Establishment of an African American Rite," in *A Survey of Opinions of African American Catholics*, ed. National Black Catholic Congress (Baltimore: National Black Catholic Congress Office, 1995), 43.

114. National Black Catholic Clergy Caucus, *Right Rites*, 4.

115. Ibid. For a fuller discussion of the integral relationship between faith and culture, see, for example, Robert J. Schreiter, *Constructing Local Theologies* (Maryknoll, N.Y.: Orbis, 1986), 159.

116. The Black bishops had already criticized the ways in which racism had "marred" U.S. evangelization efforts among Blacks. See Black Catholic Bishops of the United States, *Brothers and Sisters*, 3; Schreiter, *Local Theologies*, 144–158. Schreiter offers a detailed description of the nature of syncretism and dualism. For a description of some of the significant expressions of syncretism and dualism in the history of the Americas, see Raboteau, *Slave Religion* 16–25, 285–288.

117. Schreiter, *Local Theologies*, 150.

118. National Black Catholic Clergy Caucus, *Right Rites*.

119. National Black Catholic Congress, *A Survey of Opinions of African American Catholics* (Baltimore: National Black Catholic Congress, 1995). Forty-eight percent of the survey participants were deliberately selected from the national organizations of priests, men and women religious, deacons, and seminarians. Analysis of the survey data suggests that some of the laity who constituted the other 52 percent of respondents were not randomly selected but designated on the local level.

120. Ibid., 3.

121. Ibid., 7–16.

122. Ibid., 19–20; italics ours.

123. Ibid., 20.

124. Scott, "Canonical Reflections," 46.

125. Ibid., 50.

126. Jamie T. Phelps, "Ecclesiological Implications of 'The Study of Opinions of African American Catholics,'" in *A Survey of Opinions of African American Catholics*, 53–54.

127. Ibid., 54.

128. Ibid., 52–53, 57.

129. Diana L. Hayes, "My People Shall Never Again Be Put to Shame," in *A Survey of Opinions of African American Catholics*, 60–61.

130. Ibid., 61–64.

131. Ibid., 66.

132. Ibid., 56. Phelps summarizes and responds to some of these questions in footnote 5 of "Ecclesiological Implications."

133. The word "Afrocentricity" derives from the word "Afrology," the study of African concepts, issues, and behaviors. Molefi K. Asante, *Afrocentricity: the Theory of Social Change* (Buffalo: Amulefi, 1980), 67. Some African American scholars have reformulated the term "Afrocentricity" to "*Africentricity*" noting that this word more explicitly depicts the distinctiveness of "Africa" and encourages discussants to reflect on African culture, philosophy, and values from an emic point of view.

134. Molefi K. Asante, *Afrocentricity* (Trenton, N.J.: African World Press, 1991), and *The Afrocentric Idea* (Philadelphia: Temple University Pres, 1987).

135. See Rivers, *Soulfull Worship*; National Office for Black Catholics, *This Far by Faith*; and Posey, *Theology: Portrait in Black*.

136. Eva Marie Lumas, "The Nature and Goals of Africentric Catechesis," in *God Bless Them That Have Their Own*, ed. Therese Wilson Favors (Washington, D.C.: United States Catholic Conference of Bishops, 1995), 28–37.

137. National Black Catholic Congress, *Rise Up and Rebuild: A National Black Catholic Congress VII Follow-up Program* (Baltimore: National Black Catholic Congress Office, 1992). N.B.: Most of the innovations cited in what follows are not yet published.

138. Currently such a compilation is underway under the leadership of Ronald D. Harbor and Val Parker, in conjunction with Oregon Catholic Press, Portland, Oregon.

139. See Mary E. McGann, *A Precious Fountain: Music in the Worship of An African American Catholic Community* (Collegeville, Minn.: Liturgical Press, 2004), 23–29.

140. J-Glenn Murray, "Roots," *Plenty Good Room* (May / June 1993): 2. The journal was published by Liturgy Training Publications, Chicago.

141. Congregation for Divine Worship and the Discipline of the Sacraments, *Varietates legitimae (Inculturation and the Roman Liturgy)* (Washington, D.C.: United States Catholic Conference, 1995), no. 3.

142. Ibid., nos. 9–20.

143. Ibid., nos. 38–52.

144. Ibid., nos. 21–27, 37, 62–69.

145. Ibid., no. 34.

146. Ibid., nos. 35–36.

147. Ibid., no. 46.

148. Ibid., nos. 46–51, 54.

149. Ibid., no. 54.

150. Ibid., nos. 54–62.

151. Ibid., nos. 63, 70. The term "radical adaptations" refers to the *Constitution on the Sacred Liturgy*, no. 40.

152. Cyprian L. Rowe, "A Tale of War, A Tale of Woe," *Plenty Good Room* (September / October 1994): 11–13.

153. J-Glenn Murray, "Give and Take: A Response to War and Woe," *Plenty Good Room* (November / December 1994): 7–8. What follows in this paragraph is from the same source, 8, 10.

154. Cyprian L. Rowe, "A Tale of War, A Tale of Woe . . . Continued," *Plenty Good Room* (May / June 1996): 9–11. What follows in this paragraph is from the same source, 11–13.

155. J-Glenn Murray, "Doing the Rite Thing: A Further Response to 'War and Woe,'" *Plenty Good Room* (May / June 1996): 5–10. What follows is from the same source, 11–12.

156. Richard E. McCarron, "Response to the Tales of War and Woe," *Plenty Good Room* (September / October 1996): 4–8. Remainder of the paragraph taken from the same source, 8–9.

157. Cyprian L. Rowe, "How Long, O Lord, How Long?" *Plenty Good Room* (July / August 1997): 4. The remainder of the paragraph taken from the same source, 5–10.

158. Richard E. McCarron, "A Response to Cyprian Lamar Rowe's 'How Long, O Lord, How Long?'" *Plenty Good Room* (July / August 1997): 12; J-Glenn Murray, S.J., "A Response to Cyprian Lamar Rowe's 'How Long, O Lord, How Long?'" *Plenty Good Room* (July / August 1997): 12–13.

159. See Joseph A. Brown, "To Sit at the Welcome Table: A Meditation," *Plenty Good Room* (November / December, 1997).

160. Scott Haldeman, "Forging a New Self: A Response to War and Woe," *Plenty Good Room* (March / April 1998). Haldeman is the convener of the study group on African American Worship Traditions of the North American Academy of Liturgy.

161. Whitt, "*Varietates legitimae*," 526. What follows is taken from this source, 527, 532.

162. *Le Missel Romain pour les Diocèse du Zaïre.* See *Notitiae* 24 (1988), 454–72.

163. Whitt, "*Varietates legitimae*," 528.

164. "Vatican approves Anglican liturgy," *Tablet* (London) 239 (February 23, 1985) 198; as quoted in Whitt, 514.

165. Whitt, "*Varietates legitimae*," 534. Remainder of paragraph taken from the same source, 530–532.

166. Reference in this paragraph from ibid., 532–537.

167. See Guerin Montilus, "Culture and Faith: A Believing People," in *Tell It Like It Is: A Black Catholic Perspective on Christian Education,* ed. Eva Marie Lumas, S.S.S. (Oakland: National Black Sisters' Conference, 1983), 35–44; Black Catholic Bishops of the United States, *What We Have Seen and Heard,* 4.

168. Black Catholic Bishops of the United States, *What We Have Seen and Heard,* 8–10.

169. Based on the spiritual, "Done Made My Vow."

PART TWO   The Foundational Vision:
Clarence R. J. Rivers' Vision of Effective African American Worship

1. Insights of this chapter are based on all of Rivers' publications: *Celebration* (New York: Herder and Herder, 1969); *Soulfull Worship* (Washington, D.C.: National Office for Black Catholics, 1974); *The Spirit in Worship* (Cincinnati: Stimuli, 1978); "Music and the Liberation of Black Catholics,"

Freeing the Spirit 1, no. 1 (1971): 26–28; and "'Thank God We Ain't What We Was': The State of Liturgy in the Black Catholic Community," in *Theology: A Portrait in Black*, ed. Thaddeus Posey (Pittsburgh: The Capuchin Press, 1980), 66–74. Rivers' chapter "The Oral African Tradition Versus the Ocular Western Tradition," *The Spirit*, 16–22, was also reprinted in *Taking Down Our Harps: Black Catholics in the United States*, eds. Diana L. Hayes and Cyprian Davis (Maryknoll, N.Y.: Orbis Books, 1998), 232–246.

2. See Rivers, "'Thank God We Ain't What We Was,'" 70.

3. The term hybridity has become current in writings on bi- or pluricultural identity, but was not current when Rivers was writing. See, for example, Robert J. Schreiter, *The New Catholicity* (Maryknoll, N.Y.: Orbis Books, 2004), 74–78.

4. Aylward Shorter traces the first instance of the term inculturation to a little-known 1962 article [in French] of J. Masson. But it was well into the 1970s before the image received wider use, first in the statements of African and Asian bishops (1974), then in a letter of Father Pedro Arrupe to the Society of Jesus (1978). Its first use in a Papal document was in 1979. See Shorter, *Toward a Theology of Inculturation* (Maryknoll, N.Y.: Orbis Books, 1988), 10.

5. See Shorter, *Toward a Theology*, 13–14.

6. Rivers chose not to complete doctoral studies at the *Institut Catholique*, but earned a Ph.D. in Black Culture and Religion from the Union Graduate School of Cincinnati, and held an MA in Philosophy from the Anethaeum of Ohio. He completed graduate studies in English and American Literature at Xavier University of Cincinnati and Yale University; and graduate studies in drama at the Catholic University of America. He was a founding member of the North American Academy of Liturgy. His music has been performed by the Newport Jazz Festival and the Cincinnati Symphony Orchestra. He served as production consultant / coproducer for several documentary / TV programs for ABC and CBS. In the last several years of his life, he developed a ministerial training program entitled "Apprenticeship in Worship: Producing Worship Professionals."

7. See Rivers, *The Spirit*, 84. Rivers was a member of the Martin Luther King Fellows, an ecumenical group of ministers with whom he worked to develop models for African American Catholic prayer and preaching. Rivers

alludes to this fellowship in "Freeing the Spirit: Very Personal Reflections on One Man's Search for the Spirit in Worship," *U.S. Catholic Historian* 19, no. 2 (Spring 2001): 125–126.

8. This section is drawn from Rivers, *Celebration*, 9–39; *Soulfull Worship*, 5–10, 51–55; *The Spirit*, 34–38.

9. Rivers, *Soulfull Worship*, 51.

10. Rivers uses the term "the Black Church," "the traditional Black churches," or "Black worship," to indicate a core African religious-cultural heritage that has been preserved within African American Christianity, and which is recognizable to greater or lesser degrees in the worship of several denominations. See *The Spirit*, 25. See also Melva Costen, *African American Christian Worship* (Nashville: Abingdon Press, 1993).

11. This section is drawn from Rivers, *The Spirit*, 33–39.

12. Rivers, *The Spirit*, 37.

13. Ibid.

14. This perception is quite in contrast to Western theology's more limited focus on the role of the Holy Spirit in worship. See Kevin Irwin, *Context and Text: Method in Liturgical Theology* (Collegeville, Minn.: Liturgical Press, 1994), 48; Edward J. Kilmartin, *Christian Liturgy, Vol. I.: Systematic Theology of Liturgy* (Kansas City: Sheed and Ward, 1988), 228–232; Mary Collins, "Eucharist and Christology Revisited: The Body of Christ," *Theological Digest* 39, no. 4 (1992): 321–325.

15. This section taken from Rivers, *Soulfull Worship*, 14, and *The Spirit*, 3, 30–31, 33–3, 87–92.

16. This section based on Rivers, *The Spirit*, 10–13; 36–37; *Celebration*, 14, 29–40; *Soulfull Worship*, 51–59.

17. See John Baldovin, "The Changing World of Liturgy," *Anglican Theological Review* 82, no. 1 (Winter 2000), 66–68. Baldovin identifies a basic divide in contemporary sacramental theology, based on whether one supposes the world to be fundamentally graced or not; on whether sacraments are "a remedy for the sinfulness of the world, bringing grace where it is not," or the revelation and realization of "the graced activity of God already at work in the world." Baldovin holds that the impasse in liturgical renewal experienced in many Christian traditions—either to embrace the contemporary world or retreat from it—is intimately bound up with this

question. The cultural, sacramental perspective described by Rivers might contribute to the dialogue across this divide.

18. See Joseph A. Brown, *To Stand on the Rock: Meditations on Black Catholic Identity* (Maryknoll, N.Y.: Orbis Books, 1998), 26–27, for a fuller explanation of *àshe.*

19. Image of "fertile genius" taken from the ICEL translation of Psalm 104.

20. This section based on Rivers, *Soulfull Worship,* 15–17; *The Spirit,* 5, 30–31.

21. Text of a spiritual quoted in Rivers, *Soulfull Worship,* 17.

22. James H. Cone, "Sanctification and Liberation in the Black Religious Tradition, with Special Reference to Black Worship," in *Speaking the Truth: Ecumenism, Liberation, and Black Theology* (Maryknoll, N.Y.: Orbis Books, 1999), 20. The quote that follows is from the same source, 18.

23. This section taken from Rivers, *The Spirit,* 16–31; *Celebration,* 29–40. Rivers' perspective is reflected in *Plenty Good Room: The Spirit and Truth of African American Catholic Worship,* Secretariat for the Liturgy / Secretary for Black Catholics, National Conference of Catholic Bishops (Washington, D.C.: USCC Publications, 1991), nos. 85—87.

24. Quoted in Rivers, *The Spirit,* 17, 22. Leopold Sedar Senghor is the former poet-philosopher president of Senegal. Quote in Rivers taken from "The Psychology of the African Negro," *Freeing the Spirit,* 3, no. 3 (1974).

25. Nathan Mitchell, "God's Word: A Human Word," *Assembly* 26, no. 4 (September, 2000): 33.

26. Martha Nussbaum, *Upheavals of Thought: The Intelligence of Emotions* (Cambridge: Cambridge University Press, 2001), 1, 19, preface. The first image Nussbaum borrows from Marcel Proust.

27. See "Whatchumean, Jellybean? Or Integration in Black Catholic Ministry," in *Making a Way Out of No Way: Proceedings: Joint Conference of the National Black Sisters' Conference, National Black Catholic Clergy Caucus, the National Black Catholic Seminarians* (August, 1982), 7–8, as summarized by M. Shawn Copeland, "Method in Emerging Black Catholic Theology," in *Taking Down Our Harps: Black Catholics in the United States,* eds. Diana L. Hayes and Cyprian Davis (Maryknoll, N.Y.: Orbis Books, 1998), 127.

28. This section based primarily on Rivers, *Soulfull Worship,* 25–30; *The Spirit,* 50–61.

29. This section taken from Rivers, *The Spirit*, 25, 50–69.

30. Cyprian Davis speaks of ecstacy as "one notable characteristic of the African American contemplative experience." He notes the impact of "traditional African religion and its transplanted forms in the New World"—both of which were based upon spirit possession—on the development of African American spirituality. "Worship, including Catholic worship, is often characterized by an exuberance and vibrancy that lead to a prayer experience of tremendous joy bordering on what can only be called ecstatic. At the same time, the prayer experience . . . can become a state of meditation that is kataphatic and immediate—the crucifixion is a lived experience, the Exodus event is yesterday." See "African American Spirituality," in *The New Dictionary of Catholic Spirituality*, ed. Michael Downey (Collegeville, Minn.: Liturgical Press, 1993), 22–23.

31. For an excellent exploration of the "theodramatics" of worship, by which the human need for salvation *and* its availability are made known—clearly the theological basis of the deep spiritual renewal of which Rivers speaks—see Alex Garcia-Rivera and Tom Scirghi, *Living Beauty: A Liturgical Aesthetics* (Lanham, Md.: Rowman and Littlefield Publishers, 2007).

32. This section taken from Rivers, *Celebration*, 29–40; *The Spirit*, 50–62.

33. See Rivers, "Music and the Liberation of Black Catholics," 27–28; *Soulfull Worship*, 39–45.

34. Much emphasis has been placed in recent Roman Catholic liturgical legislation on adhering to rubrical requirements. Rivers is writing, however, in a post–Vatican II climate in which there was greater openness to local variation and a firmer commitment to the ongoing change that the *Constitution on the Sacred Liturgy* described as the "organic progression of the liturgy."

35. Rivers, *The Spirit*, 89–90.

36. What follows is taken primarily from Rivers, *The Spirit*, 16–22.

37. Here Rivers is using the term "puritanism" in a popular sense, as referring to "an extreme strictness in moral or religious matters, often to excess; a rigid austerity" (*Webster's Encyclopedic Unabridged Dictionary*), rather than as a reference to the Puritan denomination whose lives, as Martin Marty and others have pointed out, demonstrate balanced and

healthy attitudes toward sexuality. Aligning the "puritanism" with "discursiveness," Rivers is indicating a tendency to rely on the intellect, reason, and argument, while discrediting intuition, emotion, and bodily sensation.

38. Rivers, *The Spirit*, 16.

39. Rivers, *The Spirit*, 21.

40. Senghor, quoted in Rivers, *The Spirit*, 20.

41. Rivers, *The Spirit*, 17. Rivers identifies the document as coming from the Federation of Diocesan Liturgical Commissions, but gives no further details.

42. Nor is Rivers contending that persons shaped by this cultural thrust, or by the propensities of oral / aural cultures, operate exclusively according to these tendencies.

43. This section taken primarily from Rivers, *The Spirit*, 49–69.

44. Rivers, *The Spirit*, 55.

45. Rivers, *Soulfull Worship*, 55.

46. Rivers, *The Spirit*, 55.

47. See Rivers, *Soulfull Worship*, 31–38; *The Spirit*, 50–59.

48. Rivers, *The Spirit*, 57.

49. Rivers, *The Spirit*, 58.

50. This section taken from Rivers, *The Spirit*, 60–61; *Soulfull Worship*, 39–45; and "Music and the Liberation," 26–28. Rivers is at pains to delineate the varying roles of music at different moments in the Catholic liturgy, stressing that a misunderstanding of what the music is meant to do can break the dramatic flow and contribute to an aesthetic incoherence of the ritual as a whole. *The Spirit*, 60–61.

51. Rivers, *Soulfull Worship*, 39.

52. On the functional aesthetic in Black music, see Olly Wilson, "Black Music as an Art Form," *Black Music Research Journal* 3 (1983): 1–22; also Mellonee Burnim, "The Performance of Black Gospel Music as Transformation," in *Music and the Experience of God*, eds., David Power, Mary Collins, and Mellonee Burnim (Edinburgh: T. and T. Clark, Ltd., 1989), 52–61.

53. See Rivers, *Soulfull Worship*, 21, 31–45; *The Spirit*, 71–72.

54. Wyatt Tee Walker articulated these terms in *The Soul of Black Worship: Preaching, Praying, Singing* (New York: Martin Luther King Fellows Press, 1984).

55. This aesthetic is pervasive in African American artistic performance, in religious and non-religious contexts. To move others, to "have church," is an explicit goal of the Black performing arts. See, for example, Pearl Williams Jones, "Gospel Music: A Crystallization of the Black Aesthetic," *Ethnomusicology* 19, no. 3 (1975): 373–385; also Burnim, "The Performance of Gospel Music."

56. This section draws on Rivers, *The Spirit*, 72–76; 84–85; *Soulfull Worship*, 13–17; 31–36; 71–81; 83–174.

57. Rivers, *Soulfull Worship*, 14.

58. Rivers notes that this well-documented pattern of Black preaching is reflected in the patterns of Black prayer. See *The Spirit*, 72.

59. Rivers, *Soulfull Worship*, 14.

60. Rivers developed these models by inviting several Black preachers to compose a sermon on the relationship between Black culture and Catholic worship. Likewise, he asked several Black ministers to compose prayers that retain the prayer structures of Catholic liturgy while engaging the contours of Black praying. In each case, Rivers himself "absorbed" the results, adapted them to his purposes, preached and prayed them, and then composed "model" prayers and sermons that might inspire new composition within Catholic practice. See *The Spirit*, 72–76, 84–85, for his method; for models of prayers and sermons, *The Spirit*, 77–81, 87–173. His prayer models include all the presidential prayers of the eucharistic liturgy, including the eucharistic prayer. See excerpt at the end of this part.

61. See Rivers, *The Spirit*, 60–62; *Soulfull Worship*, 39–46; "Music and the Liberation," 26–28.

62. Rivers, *Soulfull Worship*, 42.

63. Rivers, *The Spirit*, ii–vi. Quotes in this paragraph taken from this source. Bishop James Lyke, O.F.M., was then president of the National Black Catholic Clergy Caucus and pastor / campus minister at Grambling State University; Joseph R. Washington, Jr., was director of Afro-American Studies and professor of Religious Studies at the University of Pennsylvania; Robert Hovda was director of the Liturgical Program, Jesuit School of Theology, Chicago, and a former staff member of the Liturgical Conference.

64. See, for example, Alyward Shorter, *Toward a Theology of Inculturation* (Maryknoll, N.Y.: Orbis Books, 1988); Anscar J. Chupungco, *Cultural*

Adaptation of the Liturgy (New York: Paulist Press, 1982); Chupungco, *Liturgies of the Future* (New York: Paulist Press, 1989); Chupungco, *Liturgical Inculturation: Sacramentals, Religiosity, and Catechesis* (Collegeville, Minn.: Liturgical Press, 1992).

65. In 1992, Anscar Chupungco would write, "The history of the liturgy attests to the Church's creative skill in shaping new rites in order to transmit the message in ways that could be understood and appreciated by the worshiping community. One of the ways favored by the council is the dynamic translation of the Roman liturgy, or inculturation, whereby the original content of the rite is preserved. But Christian life is richer in content and scope than the Roman liturgy. There is more to life than what the Roman formularies and rites are able to embody. In short, inculturation [as circumscribed by this understanding] cannot fully satisfy all the requirements for a truly renewed liturgy of a local Church. Creativity . . . is sometimes not a mere option but an imperative for a local Church that wants its liturgy to be relevant and have impact on the life of the faithful"; *Liturgical Inculturation*, 53–54.

66. Shorter, in *Toward a Theology*, 13–14, drawing on a word coined by Bishop Joseph Blomjous in 1980, speaks of any attempts at inculturation as such a two-way dialogue—a true "interculturation," in which "the Christian message transforms culture" and "Christianity is transformed" in turn, by culture. The fruit is that "the message is formulated and interpreted anew."

67. In a 1998 article, Peter Phan contends that, in a time of contentious discussion of what constitutes unity in the Church, a true unity-in-diversity must be rooted in a commitment to "enable God's *salvation* in Christ to reach as many persons as possible," while being "as diverse as possible in choosing the *ways* and *means* to achieve this goal." His proposal is in keeping with Rivers' focus on "effective" worship. See Phan, "How Much Uniformity Can We Stand? How Much Unity Do We Want?" *Worship* 72, no. 3, reprinted in *Being Religious Interreligiously*, 253–254.

68. Rivers, *The Spirit*, iv.

69. See Mary E. McGann, *A Precious Fountain: Music in the Worship of an African American Catholic Community* (Collegeville, Minn.: Liturgical Press, 2004), which documents the life and liturgy of Our Lady of Lourdes, a Black Catholic community in San Francisco. Our Lady of Lourdes is but one of

many that imbue the ideals that Rivers holds out. See especially Ronald D. Harbor, "Constructing an African American Catholic Aesthetic: Ways and Means of Negotiating the Amens in the Liturgical Assembly," M.T.S. Thesis, Franciscan School of Theology, 2001, which focuses on the neighboring community of St. Columba's, Oakland, California.

70. See, for example, McGann, *A Precious Fountain*, 195–196.

71. See Rivers, "'Thank God We Ain't What We Was,'" 73.

72. Rivers, *The Spirit*, iii.

73. For example, although Clarence Rivers was a founding member of the North American Academy of Liturgy, its first study group on African American worship traditions was founded only six years ago, and remains small. See also the striking presidential address given by Jon Nilson to the Catholic Theological Society of America, in which he states that while Catholic theologians have embraced other liberation theologies, they have yet to truly engage Black theology. Nilson, "Confessions of a White Racist Catholic Theologian," *Catholic Theological Society of America Proceedings*, 58 (2003): 64–82.

74. Rivers, from his sermon, "Worship in Spirit and Truth," *The Spirit*, 90–92.

75. This eucharistic prayer in its completeness follows the normal structure of Roman Catholic Prayers, with portions such as the "Words of Institution" identical to the approved texts; taken from Rivers, *The Spirit*, 78–81.

PART THREE   **Aesthetic Principles:**

Constructing an African American Catholic Liturgical Aesthetic

1. The work of constructing this liturgical aesthetic began in the lived practice of one predominantly African American Catholic community in Oakland, Calif. See Ronald D. Harbor, "Constructing an African American Catholic Aesthetic: Ways and Means of Negotiating the Amens in the Liturgical Assembly," M.T.S. Thesis, Franciscan School of Theology, Berkeley, Calif. (2001).

2. At the time of the 1978 symposium, Bishop Braxton had not yet been ordained a bishop.

3. The first Black Catholic Theological Symposium was held in Baltimore, Md., October 12–15, 1978. Of the thirty-three participants, twelve

scholars gave major presentations on Black values, Black self-concept, liturgical celebration, spirituality, pastoral theology, and catechetics.

4. Although the National Conference of Catholic Bishops has published two documents on liturgy in the African American Catholic community, *In Spirit and Truth* (1987) and *Plenty Good Room* (1990), neither of these documents contain any bibliographic references to the 1978 Black Catholic Theological Symposium.

5. Clarence-Rufus J. Rivers, "Freeing the Spirit: Very Personal Reflections on One Man's Search for the Spirit in Worship" (Cincinnati, Ohio: Stimuli, Inc.: 2001), 56 pages. A large excerpt of this article was published in *U.S. Historian* 19, no. 2 (Spring 2001): 95–143. This article chronicles Father Rivers' journey through his formation as a liturgist, formative attitudes on music in liturgy, initial attempts in liturgical adaptation, and his overall interest in the drama of worship. It was in 1956 that he began to contemplate the importance of Black music in the Catholic Church and its special benefit to African American assemblies like St. Joseph's.

6. "Freeing the Spirit," 19.

7. See Rivers, "'Thank God We Ain't What We Was': The State of Liturgy in the Black Catholic Community," in *Theology: A Portrait in Black: Proceedings of the 1978 Black Catholic Theological Symposium,* ed. Thaddeus J. Posey, O.F.M. Cap. (Washington, D.C.: National Black Clergy Caucus, 1980), 68.

8. Thaddeus J. Posey, O.F.M. Cap., ed., *Theology: A Portrait in Black: Proceedings of the 1978 Black Catholic Theological Symposium* (Washington, D.C.: National Black Clergy Caucus, 1980).

9. A distillation of sacramental theology, catechesis, African and African American history, performative elements in liturgical assemblies (singing, preaching, movement, praising, proclamation), liturgics, psychology of belief, scripture, health (mental and physical), civic sense of obligation, vocation and formation, sacramental initiation, ethics (religious and civil), and social justice concerns.

10. Educational theorists had begun to explore the impact of varied teaching methodologies and the "hidden" curriculum, such as the art used in the educational environment, on the effectiveness learning.

11. Dr. Toinette Eugene has served as provost and professor of social ethics at Colgate Rochester Theological Seminary (Rochester, N.Y.), as

professor of social ethics at Garrett Theological Seminary (Evanston, Ill.), and as director of the African American Catholic Pastoral Center in the diocese of Oakland, Calif. At the time of the symposium, she was a Ph.D. candidate.

12. Toinette Eugene, "Developing Black Catholic Belief: Catechesis as a Black Articulation of the Faith," in Posey, *Portrait in Black,* 140–159.

13. This interdependent relationship has been reiterated by numerous current authors who underscore the formative and educative role of Catholic worship. See Gilbert Ostdiek, *Catechesis for Liturgy* (Washington, D.C.: Pastoral Press, 1986); Michael Warren, *Faith, Culture, and the Worshiping Community: Shaping the Practice of the Local Church,* revised edition (New York, N.Y.: Paulist Press, 1993); Maria Harris, *Fashion Me a People: Curriculum in the Church* (Louisville, Ky.: Westminster, 1989); Nathan Jones, *Crossing Over: Teaching and Celebrating the Sacraments in Black Churches* (Chicago, Ill.: Ethnic Communications Outlet, 1983).

14. Eugene, 142.

15. Ibid., 141.

16. Ibid., 142.

17. See Part One of this volume.

18. Eugene, 146.

19. Ibid., 144.

20. Ibid., 146.

21. Alfred North Whitehead, *Symbolism* (Cambridge: Oxford University Press, 1927), 88. As quoted in Eugene, 147.

22. Eugene, 149. Material in this paragraph taken from 149–150, 152.

23. Ibid., 155.

24. These conclusions are taken from Eugene, 155–156.

25. In 1978, Edward Kenneth Braxton was assistant chancellor for theological affairs in the diocese of Cleveland, Ohio, as well as a visiting professor of theology at the University of Notre Dame. After a short pastorship of his home parish in Chicago, Ill., he was made auxiliary bishop of the archdiocese of Saint Louis, Mo., and, in 2001, was named ordinary of the diocese of Lake Charles, La.

26. Edward K. Braxton, "Religion, Values, Ethnicity and the Black Experience," in Posey, *Portrait in Black,* 15–30. Father Braxton's presentation to

the symposium was not developed as a "formal paper," but was included in the symposium proceedings as a transcription of his oral presentation. Hence, it is missing the citations that would normally accompany such a symposium paper.

27. This section does not exhaust the topics covered in Braxton's presentation.

28. Braxton, 28.

29. Braxton, 30.

30. Reflections in this paragraph taken from Braxton, 16.

31. Reflections in this paragraph taken from Braxton, 16–17.

32. Braxton, 16.

33. Ibid.

34. Ibid.

35. Ibid., 17.

36. The image is based on the root meaning of *lietourgía* as the "work of the people."

37. Reflections and quotes in this paragraph taken from Braxton, 18.

38. Reflections and quotes in this paragraph taken from Braxton, 18.

39. Reflections and quotes in this paragraph taken from Braxton, 18–19.

40. Reflections and quotes in this paragraph taken from Braxton, 19.

41. Quotes and reflections regarding the aesthetic pattern taken from Braxton, 19–20.

42. Quotes and reflections regarding the dramatic pattern taken from Braxton, 20.

43. Quotes and reflections regarding the mystical pattern taken from Braxton, 21.

44. Howard Thurman, *Meditations of the Heart* (New York, N.Y.: Harper and Row, 1953), 48.

45. Cyprian Davis, "African American Spirituality," in Michael Downey, ed., *The New Dictionary of Catholic Spirituality* (Collegeville, Minn.: Liturgical Press, 1993), 22.

46. Christian Koontz, R.S.M., ed., *Thea Bowman: Handing on Her Legacy* (Kansas City, Mo.: Sheed & Ward, 1991), 5.

47. Reflections and quotes that follow taken from Braxton, 21.

48. Quotes in this paragraph from Braxton, 21.

49. Braxton, 18.

50. Reflections and quotes on the six modes of conversion taken from Braxton, 21–23.

51. Reflections and quotes in this paragraph taken from Braxton, 21.

52. Braxton, 24–25.

53. Reflections in this paragraph taken from Braxton, 25.

54. Braxton makes reference to the Hispanic theology of Gustavo Gutierrez and the feminist theology of Mary Daly, as well as the Black theology of James Cone, Major Jones, Eulalio Baltazar, Deotis Roberts, "and many others"; Braxton, 25–26.

55. Braxton, 26. What follows is from that page.

56. Braxton distinguishes a "classic" from a "period piece" in that the latter, although a work of interest, value, and significance, is not of perennial worth. Reflections and quotes in this section from Braxton, 29–30.

57. Braxton, 30. Italics mine.

58. At the time of the symposium, Glenn Jean-Marie was a priest of the archdiocese of New Orleans and pastor of St. Augustine Catholic Church. In the early 1990s, his quest to wed the principles of an emerging African American Catholic theology with American Catholicism led him to join Archbishop George Stallings in the foundation of Imani Temple in 1991. Jean-Marie's untimely death in January, 1993, was a loss to the whole Black Catholic community.

59. Glenn V. Jean-Marie, "Black Catholic Worship: Celebrating Roots and Wings," in Posey, *Theology: A Portrait in Black*, 75–90.

60. Ibid., 75. Quotes and reflections in this paragraph taken from Jean-Marie, 75–76. Note that in Jean-Marie's presentation, many words are capitalized for emphasis. Quotations here reflect his capitalization.

61. Jean-Marie, 76.

62. Ibid., 82.

63. Ibid., 76.

64. Quotes and reflections in this paragraph taken from Jean-Marie, 76–78.

65. Quotes and reflections in this paragraph taken from Jean-Marie, 76, 82.

66. Jean-Marie, 82.

67. As quoted in Jean-Marie, 79–80.

68. Robert Pollock, ed., *The Mind of Pius XII* (New York: Crown Publishers, Inc., 1955), 91; as quoted in Jean-Marie, 78.

69. *The Teachings of Pope Paul—1969* (Vatican: Liberia Editrice Vaticana), 204; as quoted in Jean-Marie, 79.

70. See nos. 36–40 of Vatican II's *Constitution on the Sacred Liturgy*.

71. Jean-Marie, 80.

72. Quotes and reflections that follow taken from Jean-Marie, 80–81.

73. Jean-Marie, 81.

74. Quotes in this paragraph taken from Jean-Marie, 81–82.

75. Quote and reflections which follow taken from Jean-Marie, 83–85.

76. *Decree on the Ministry and life of Priests*, 4.

77. Jean-Marie, 84–85.

78. What follows is drawn from Jean-Marie, 85–88.

79. The structure and flow of this prayer are identical to that of other approved Catholic eucharistic prayers. The *epiclesis* and "Words of Institution" are also identical to those of approved prayers, and other phraseology from approved prayer texts is interwoven with the imagery and metaphors of Black prayer discourse.

80. M. Shawn Copeland, "Foundations for Catholic Theology in an African American Context," in *Black and Catholic: The Challenge and Gift of Black Folk*, ed. Jamie Phelps (Milwaukee: Marquette University Press, 1997), 138.

81. Excerpt from "O God, Our Help in Ages Past," composed by eighteenth-century hymn writer Isaac Watts (1674–1748), whose hymn compositions are often referred to by Black communities as "Dr. Watts."

82. Again, a reference to the hymn "Amazing Grace," composed by John Newton (1725–1807) and beloved of African American communities.

83. Jean-Marie, 85–87.

84. Ibid., 87.

85. Ibid., 87–88.

86. Quotes and reflections in this paragraph from Jean-Marie, 88.

87. Rivers, "'Thank God We Ain't What We Was': The State of the Liturgy in the Black Catholic Community," in *Theology: Portrait in Black*, 66–74.

88. See Part Two of this volume for a full account of Rivers' publications.

89. Quotes and reflections in this paragraph from Rivers, 66.

90. Rivers does not cite his source.

91. Quotes and reflections in this paragraph from Rivers, 67–68.

92. Ibid., 70.

93. Telephone interviews with Father Rivers, April 28, May 1, 2001. What follows in this and the following paragraph taken from the same source, unless otherwise noted.

94. Rivers, *Theology: A Portrait in Black,* 70.

95. Ibid, 70.

96. Ibid., 71. Rivers is referring here to a current ecclesial document from the American Bishops that addressed the problem of poor preaching in Catholic communities with the development of a new "theology of preaching."

97. Unless otherwise noted, remainder of paragraph from telephone interview.

98. Rivers, *Theology: A Portrait in Black,* 71.

99. Ibid., 72.

100. Ibid., 73.

101. Quotes and reflections in this section from Rivers, *Theology: A Portrait in Black,* 73.

102. Rivers speaks of this explicitly in *Soulfull Worship* (Washington, D.C.: National Office for Black Catholics, 1974), 17.

103. Ibid., 25.

104. Ibid., 17.

105. Quotes in this paragraph from Jean-Marie, 80, 83.

106. Based on Eugene, 141.

107. Braxton, 30.

Contributors

1. *A Precious Fountain* was awarded first place in Liturgy in the Catholic Press Association's 2005 Book Awards.

SELECT BIBLIOGRAPHY

Abbington, James, ed. *Readings in African American Church Music and Worship*. Chicago: GIA, 2001.

Allen, Ray. "Shouting the Church: Narrative and Vocal Improvisation in African American Gospel Quartet Performance." *Journal of American Folklore* 104, no. 413 (1991): 295–317.

Bauer, Hans A. *African American Religion: Varieties of Protest and Accommodation*. Knoxville: University of Tennessee Press, 2002.

Black Catholic Bishops, National Conference of Catholic Bishops. *"What We Have Seen and Heard": A Pastoral Letter on Evangelization from the Black Catholic Bishops of the United States*. Cincinnati: St. Anthony Messenger Press, 1984.

Bowman, Thea. "The Gift of African American Sacred Song." In *Lead Me, Guide Me*. Chicago: G.I.A. Publications, 1987.

———. "Black History and Culture." *U.S. Catholic Historian* 7, no. 2–3 (1988): 307–310.

———. "Justice, Power, and Praise." In *Liturgy and Social Justice*, ed. Edward M. Grosz. Collegeville, Minn.: Liturgical Press, 1989.

———. "To Be Black and Catholic." *Origins* 19, no. 8 (1989).

Braxton, Edward K. "We, Too, Sing America." In *Our Roots and Gifts*, 80–101. Washington, D.C.: Office of Black Catholics, 1989.

———. *The Faith Community: One, Holy, Catholic and Apostolic*. Notre Dame: Ave Maria Press, 1990.

Brown, Joseph A. *To Stand on the Rock: Meditations on Black Catholic Identity.* Maryknoll, N.Y.: Orbis, 1998.

Burnim, Mellonee. "The Performance of Black Gospel Music as Transformation." In *Music and the Experience of God,* ed. David Power et al., 52–61. Edinburgh: T. and T. Clark, 1989.

Carter, Harold A. *The Prayer Tradition of Black People.* Valley Forge: Judson Press, 1976.

Cepress, Celestine. *Sister Thea Bowman, Shooting Star: Selected Writings and Speeches.* Winona, Minn.: St. Mary's Press, Christian Brothers Publications, 1993.

Conwill, Giles. "The Word Became Black Flesh." In *Evangelizing Blacks,* ed. Glen C. Smith, 45–72. New York: Paulist Press, 1988.

Cooper-Lewter, Nicholas C., and Henry H. Mitchell. *Soul Theology: The Heart of American Black Culture.* San Francisco: Harper and Row, 1986.

Copeland, Shawn M. "African American Catholics and Black Theology: An Interpretation." In *Black Theology: A Documentary History. Vol. II: 1980–1992,* ed. James H. Cone and Gayraud S. Wilmore. Maryknoll, N.Y.: Orbis, 1993.

Costen, Melva W. *African American Christian Worship.* Second edition. Nashville, Tenn.: Abingdon, 2007.

———. *In Spirit and in Truth: The Music of African American Worship.* Louisville: Westminister / John Knox Press, 2004.

Costen, Melva W., ed. *African American Worship: Faith Looking Forward.* Vol. 27. Atlanta: *Journal of the Interdenominational Theological Center,* 2000.

Costen, Melva W., and Darius Leander Swann, ed. *The Black Christian Worship Experience.* Vol. 4, Black Church Scholars Series. Atlanta: Interdenominational Theological Center Press, 1992.

Davis, Cyprian. "The Black Catholic Community." *U.S. Catholic Historian* 5, no. 1 (1988): 1–18.

———. "Evangelization and Culture in the Historical Context of Black America." In *Our Roots and Gifts,* 109–114. Washington, D.C.: Archdiocese of Washington, 1989.

———. *The History of Black Catholics in the United States.* New York: Crossroad, 1990.

———. "African American Spirituality." In *The New Dictionary of Catholic Spirituality*, ed. Michael Downey. Collegeville, Minn.: Liturgical Press, 1993.

———. "The Future of African American Catholic Studies." *U.S. Catholic Historian* 12, no. 2 (1994): 1–10.

Dillard, J. L. *Black English: Its History and Usage in the United States*. New York: Random House, 1972.

Egbulem, Nwaka Chris. *The Power of Africentric Celebrations: Inspirations from the Zairean Liturgy*. New York: Crossroad, 1996.

Eugene, Toinette M. "Between 'Lord, Have Mercy!' and 'Thank You, Jesus!'" In *Taking Down Our Harps: Black Catholic in the United States*, ed. Diana L. Hayes and Cyprian Davis. Maryknoll, N.Y.: Orbis, 1998.

Franklin, Robert Michael. *Liberating Visions: Human Fulfillment and Social Justice in African American Thought*. Minneapolis: Fortress Press, 1990.

———. "Defiant Spirituality: Worship and Formation in the Black Churches." *Proceedings of the North American Academy of Liturgy* (1992).

Gregory, Wilton D. "Black Catholic Liturgy: What Do You Say It Is?" *U.S. Catholic Historian* 7, no. 2–3 (1988): 316–319.

Harbor, Ronald D. "Constructing an African American Catholic Aesthetic: Ways and Means of Negotiating the Amens in the Liturgical Assembly." M.T.S. thesis, Franciscan School of Theology, 2001.

Hayes, Diana L. "Black Catholic Revivalism: The Emergence of a New Form of Worship." *Journal of the Interdenominational Theological Center* 14 (1986/1987).

———. "Tracings of an American Theology: A Black Catholic Perspective." In *Our Roots and Gifts*. Washington, D.C.: National Office of Black Catholics, 1989.

———. *Let Us Go Rejoicing: An Historical and Theological Reflection on Rejoice! Black Catholic Conference on Liturgy*. Washington, D.C.: Archdiocese of Washington Office of Black Catholics, 1990.

———. "Response to Reginald Whitt, 'Not Rite Now'." *Church* (1990).

———. "An African American Catholic Rite: Questions of Inculturation, Collegiality, and Subsidiarity." *Living Light* (1992).

———. "Should Black Catholics Have a Rite of Their Own?" *U.S. Catholic* (1992).

————. "An African American Catholic Rite: Possibilities and Perils."
Anima: Journal on Liturgy and Spirituality 17 (1993).

————. "Slain in the Spirit: Black Americans and the Holy Spirit." *Journal
of the Interdenominational Theological Center* 20, no. 1–2 (1993).

————. "To Be Black, Catholic, and Female." *New Theology Review* 6, no. 2
(1993): 55–62.

————. "My People Shall Never Again Be Put to Shame." In *A Survey of
Opinions of African American Catholics,* ed. National Black Catholic
Congress. Baltimore: National Black Catholic Congress Office, 1995.

————. *Trouble Don't Last Always: Soul Prayers.* Collegeville, Minn.: Liturgical Press, 1995.

————. *And We Shall Rise: An Introduction to Black Liberation Theology.* New
York: Paulist Press, 1996.

Hayes, Diana L., and Cyprian Davis, eds. *Taking Down Our Harps.* Maryknoll, N.Y.: Orbis, 1998.

Hopkins, Dwight N., and George C. L. Cummings, eds. *Cut Loose Your Stam-
mering Tongue: Black Theology in the Slave Narratives.* Louisville:
Westminster / John Knox Press, 2003.

John Paul II, Pope. "Address to Black Catholic Leadership in New Orleans."
In *Unity in the Work of Service.* Washington, D.C.: National Conference
of Catholic Bishops, 1987.

Jones, Arthur. *Wade in the Water: The Wisdom of the Spirituals.* Maryknoll:
Orbis Press, 1993.

Koontz, Christian. *Thea Bowman: Handing on Her Legacy.* Kansas City, Mo.:
Sheed and Ward, 191.

Lincoln, C. Eric, ed. *The Black Experience in Religion.* Garden City, N.Y.:
Anchor Press, 1974.

Lincoln, C. Eric. *Race, Religion and the Continuing American Dilemma.* Rev.
ed. New York: Hill and Wang, 1999.

Lincoln, C. Eric, and Lawrence H. Mamiya. *The Black Church in the African
American Experience.* Durham: Duke University Press, 1990.

Lumbala, Francois Kabasele. *The Imprint of the Human on Christian Worship.*
Dublin: Societas Liturgica, Congress XV, 1995.

Lyke, James P. "Black Liturgy / Black Liberation." *Freeing the Spirit* 1, no. 1
(1971): 14–17.

———. "Application of Black Cultural Considerations to Catholic Worship." In *This Far by Faith*. Washington, D.C.: Liturgical Conference, 1977.

———. "Liturgical Expression in the Black Community." *Worship* 57, no. 1 (1983): 14–33.

MacGregor, Morris J. *The Emergence of a Black Catholic Community: St. Augustine's in Washington*. Washington, D.C.: Catholic University of America Press, 1999.

Maultsby, Portia, and Mellonee Burnim. *African American Music: An Anthology*. New York: Routledge, 2005.

McClain, William B. "The Black Religious Experience in the United States." In *This Far by Faith*. Washington, D.C.: Liturgical Conference, 1977.

McGann, Mary E. "Timely Wisdom, Prophetic Challenge: Rediscovering Clarence R. J. Rivers' Vision of Effective Worship." *Worship* 76, no. 1 (2002): 2–24.

———. *A Precious Fountain: Music in the Worship of an African American Catholic Community*. Virgil Michel Series, ed. Don E. Saliers. Collegeville, Minn.: Liturgical Press, 2004.

McGann, Mary E., and Eva Marie Lumas. "The Emergence of African American Catholic Worship." *U.S. Catholic Historian* 19, no. 2 (2001): 27–65.

Mitchell, Henry H. *Black Preaching: The Recovery of a Powerful Art*. Nashville: Abingdon, 1991.

National Black Catholic Congress, Inc. *A Study of Opinions of African American Catholics*. Baltimore: National Black Catholic Congress, 1995.

National Conference of Catholic Bishops. *Brothers and Sisters to Us All: U.S. Bishops' Pastoral Letter on Racism in Our Day*. Washington, D.C.: United States Catholic Conference, 1979.

National Conference of Catholic Bishops, Secretariat for Black Catholics, and Secretariat for the Liturgy. *Plenty Good Room: The Spirit and Truth of African American Catholic Worship*. Washington, D.C.: United States Catholic Conference, 1990.

National Conference of Catholic Bishops, Secretariat for the Liturgy, Black Liturgy Subcommittee. *In Spirit and Truth: Black Catholic Reflections on the Order of Mass*. Washington, D.C.: United States Catholic Conference, 1987.

National Office of Black Catholics, Liturgical Conference, ed. *This Far by Faith: American Black Worship and Its African Roots.* Washington, D.C.: National Office for Black Catholics, 1977.

Ochs, Stephen J. *Desegregating the Altar: The Josephites and the Struggle for Black Priests, 1871–1960.* Baton Rouge: Louisiana State Press, 1990.

Office of Worship, Archdiocese of Washington, D. C., ed. *Our Roots and Gifts: Evangelization and Culture: An African American Catholic Perspective.* Washington, D.C.: Office of Black Catholics, 1989.

Paul VI, Pope. "The African Church Today." *The Pope Speaks* 14, no. 3 (1969): 214–220.

Phelps, Jamie T. "Black Spirituality." In *Spiritual Traditions for the Contemporary Church*, ed. Robin Mass and Gabriel O'Donnell. Nashville, Tenn.: Abingdon, 1990.

———. "The Theology and Process of Inculturation." *New Theology Review* 7, no. 1 (1994): 5–13.

———. "Ecclesiological Implications of 'The Study of Opinions of African American Catholics'." In *A Study of Opinions of African American Catholics.* Baltimore: National Black Catholic Congress, 1995.

Phelps, Jamie T., ed. *Black and Catholic: The Challenge and Gift of Black Folk.* Milwaukee: Marquette University Press, 1997.

Pitts, Walter F. *Old Ship of Zion: The Afro-Baptist Ritual in the African Diaspora.* New York: Oxford University Press, 1993.

Posey, Thaddeus J., ed. *Theology: A Portrait in Black: Black Catholic Theological Symposium.* Pittsburgh: Capuchin Press, 1980.

Raboteau, Albert J. *Slave Religion: The "Invisible Institution" in the Antebellum South.* New York: Oxford University Press, 1978.

———. *Religion and the Slave Family in the Antebellum South.* Notre Dame: University of Notre Dame Press, 1980.

———. *A Fire in the Bones: Reflections on African American Religious History.* Boston: Beacon Press, 1995.

———. *Canaan Land: A Religious History of African Americans.* New York: Oxford University Press, 2001.

Reagon, Bernice Johnson. "Let the Church Sing 'Freedom'." *Black Music Research Journal* 7 (1987): 105–18.

———. *We'll Understand It Better By and By: Pioneering African American Gospel Composers.* Washington, D.C.: Smithsonian Institution Press, 1992.

Rivers, Clarence R. J. *Reflections.* New York: Herder and Herder, 1970.

———. *Soulfull Worship.* Washington, D.C.: National Office for Black Catholics, 1974.

———. *The Spirit in Worship.* Cincinnati: Stimuli, Inc, 1978.

———. "Freeing the Spirit: Very Personal Reflections on One Man's Search for the Spirit in Worship." *U.S. Catholic Historian* 19, no. 2 (2001): 95–143.

Roberts, Leon C. "The Development of African American Liturgical Music since Vatican II." In *Our Roots and Gifts.* Washington, D.C.: National Office of Black Catholics, 1989.

Rowe, Cyprian L. "The Case for a Distinctive Black Culture." In *This Far by Faith: American Black Worship and Its African Roots,* ed. National Office of Black Catholics. Washington, D.C.: The Liturgical Conference, 1977.

Sanders, Cheryl Jeanne. *Saints in Exile: The Holiness-Pentecostal Experience in African American Religion and Culture.* New York: Oxford University Press, 1996.

Scott, Leonard G. "Canonical Reflections on the Study Conducted by the National Black Catholic Congress Regarding the Establishment of an African American Rite." In *A Survey of Opinions of African American Catholics,* ed. National Black Catholic Congress. Baltimore: National Black Catholic Congress Office, 1995.

Sernett, Milton C. *Bound for the Promised Land: African American Religion and the Great Migration.* Durham: Duke University Press, 1997.

Sharpes, Ronald L. "The Emergence of Black Cultural Expression in the Roman Catholic Liturgy." M.A. thesis, American University, 1985.

———. "Black Catholics in the United States: A Historical Chronology." *U.S. Catholic Historian* 12, no. 1 (1994): 119–141.

———. "Black Catholic Gifts of Faith." *U.S. Catholic Historian* 15, no. 4 (1997): 29–55.

Sobel, Mechal. *The World They Made Together: Black and White Values in Eighteenth-Century Virginia.* Princeton, N.J.: Princeton University Press, 1987.

————. *Trabelin' On: The Slave Journey to an Afro-Baptist Faith*. Rev. ed. Princeton, N.J.: Princeton University Press, 1988.

Thompson, Robert Farris. *Flash of the Spirit: African and Afro-American Art and Philosophy*. New York: Random House, 1983.

Washington, James Melvin. *Conversations with God: Two Centuries of Prayers by African Americans*. New York: HarperPerennial, 1995.

Weisenfeld, Judith. *African American Women and Christian Activism: New York's Black YWCA, 1905–1945*. Cambridge, Mass.: Harvard University Press, 1997.

Whitt, D. R. "Not Rite Now: An African American Church?" *Church* (Spring, 1990): 5–10.

————. "*Varietates Legitimae* and an African American Liturgical Tradition." *Worship* 71, no. 6 (1997): 504–537.

Mary E. McGann, R.S.C.J., Ph.D., is associate professor of liturgy and music at the Franciscan School of Theology and a member of the doctoral faculty at the Graduate Theological Union, Berkeley, California. For over a decade, her research has focused on African American Catholic worship, particularly on the impact of Black gospel music on the celebration of Catholic liturgy. She is the author of award-winning[1] *A Precious Fountain: Music in the Worship of an African American Catholic Community* (Collegeville, Minn.: Liturgical Press, 2004), a work of liturgical ethnography that documents her ten-year association with the Our Lady of Lourdes community, a predominantly African American Catholic parish in San Francisco, as well as *Exploring Music as Worship and Theology* (Collegeville, Minn.: Liturgical Press, 2002). She holds a Ph.D. in Worship, Proclamation and the Arts from the Graduate Theological Union, with studies in ethnomusicology at the University of California, Berkeley.

Eva Marie Lumas, S.S.S., D.Min., is assistant professor of faith formation and culture, and codirector of the Master of Arts in Ministry for a Multicultural Church at the Franciscan School of Theology, Berkeley, California. She is an associate director of the Institute for Black Catholic Studies at Xavier University of Louisiana; cofounder of *the Catechist Formation Program* at that same institute; director of *Sankofa Works*, a faith-development, pastoral training, and resource network for the African American community; and codirector of *Godworks*, a training and resource network for liturgy in the Black Catholic community. Eva Marie has served as consultant for religious education in the Black community in the archdioceses of Los Angeles and Oakland, California; as director of religious education programs for the National Black Sisters' Conference; and as associate pastor and coordinator of liturgy at St. Columba Catholic Church, Oakland, California. She has conducted numerous workshops throughout the United States on such topics as inculturation, Africentric religious education, liturgy in the Black community, liturgical catechesis, and evangelization. Eva Marie holds a Doctorate of Ministry degree from Howard University, Washington, D.C.

Ronald Dean (Rawn) Harbor, M.T.S., is coordinator of liturgy and music at the Franciscan School of Theology, Berkeley, California; liturgist at St. Columba's Parish, Oakland, California; and adjunct instructor in pastoral ministry at the Institute for Black Catholic Studies at Xavier University, New Orleans. Since 1974, Rawn has offered lectures / workshops across the United States on worship and music in the African American community. He has served as director of the office of worship for the diocese of Wichita, Kansas; as consultant in liturgy and music to Holy Savior Church and School in that same city; and has taught and founded gospel choirs in several university settings, including the University of San Francisco. Rawn was a member of the editorial team for *Lead Me, Guide Me Hymnal* and is currently the chief coordinator of work on its sequel, the *Psalmody Project*. He recently completed work on the Lutheran Synod sacramental music project, including publication of several of his psalms in the hymnal *This Far by Faith*. His "Mass of Liberation" was published in 2005. Rawn holds a Masters in Theological Studies from the Franciscan School of Theology at the Graduate Theological Union, Berkeley, California.

INDEX

African American Catholic bishops, 9, 16, 17, 22, 26, 29, 141 (n. 28), 147 (n.116)
  and creation of national offices, 22
  Black Liturgy Subcommittee, 22, 30
  Secretariat for Black Catholics, 22
  Standing Committee for Black Catholics, 22
  and evangelization, 17
African American Catholic faith, life, culture, x
  as "classic"expressions of Catholic tradition, 106, 131
  and dignity of Black humanity, 107, 116, 125
  and negative Black identity, 6
African American Catholic liturgical aesthetic. *See* liturgical aesthetic
African American Catholic parishes, 10, 15, 20–22, 35–36, 122
  in *Fire in the Pews*, 20–22
  and white clerical leadership, 10

African American Catholic rite, 15–17, 24–28, 29, 33, 34–39, 48–50
African American Catholic theologians, xii, 9, 17, 29, 32, 45, 78, 81, 127
African American Catholic worship/ liturgy, xii, xiii, 28, 29, 30, 31, 40, 61, 115
  assembly, role of, 31, 60, 64–65, 73, 75, 76, 79, 111, 120, 123–25, 128, 129, 130
  as prime witness of the faith, 64–65, 128
  as "authentically Black and truly Catholic," 15, 17–18, 22, 30, 51
  and biblical faith, 61–62
  Black cultural idiom in, 18, 108–9
  catharsis in, 65–66, 71, 73
  as drama, dramatic structure of, 8, 12, 21, 25, 56, 64–69, 71–77, 122, 128
  as effective liturgy. *See* effective worship

as embodied, holistic, xi, 13, 18, 21,
    30, 60, 75, 96, 98, 120, 122
emotion in, 19, 31, 63–64, 66,
    67–71, 72, 73, 76, 122, 128
as enriched by art forms of the Black
    Church, 12, 21, 56, 75–78, 127
environment for, 14, 20, 79, 128
eucharistic prayer texts for, 15, 28,
    76, 82–84, 112–14, 115, 119
excellence in all dimensions of, 28,
    31, 73, 76, 119–22, 130
as fusion of horizons, 55
gospel metanoia evoked in, 57,
    65–66, 71–73, 75, 121
Holy Spirit, presence in, 58–60, 62,
    64, 65–66, 67, 71–78, 81, 82–84,
    91, 111, 113, 116, 120–21, 122–24,
    126, 129
as improvisatory, free, and related to
    life, xii, 8, 14, 19, 20, 30, 31, 57,
    67, 107, 108, 119, 122
language of, including Black verbal
    arts, 24, 28, 31, 40, 76, 93, 110,
    112–14, 116, 124, 126, 127
liturgical ministers, 9–10, 15, 40, 41,
    90, 116, 120
    charism and competence of,
        64–65, 123, 127–28, 130, 131
    as instruments of the Holy Spirit,
        120, 124
and metanoia, 57, 65–66, 71, 73, 75,
    78, 121
music as central to, 8, 11–12, 13, 18,
    19, 20–21, 23, 24, 35, 40, 56, 59,
    74–76, 77, 93, 107, 118–20, 126,
    127, 128, 129

oral/aural predilections of, 13, 24,
    67–71
as pastoral priority, 121
as participatory, dialogic, poly-
    phonic, 31, 64, 91, 125–26
performative approach to, xiv, xiv,
    56, 58–78, 79, 87–89, 104, 107,
    115, 119, 120, 125–32
poetic, aesthetic coherence of,
    74–75, 119–20
praying, proclaiming, preaching,
    praising, as critical elements of,
    111, 114, 116
preaching in, 5, 8, 13, 14, 15, 18–20,
    21, 24, 31, 72, 75–76, 110–12, 116,
    119–20, 125, 128–29
    special urgency in Black commu-
        nity, 21, 112
prophetic leadership of, xiii, xiv, 6,
    9, 16, 22–23
ritual emphases of, 31
and sacramental sensibilities,
    cultural intuitions, xii, 4, 13, 18,
    40, 57, 60–61, 68, 75
sacred and secular, perceptions of,
    18, 60–61, 110
sensorium of engagement in, 31, 42,
    61
spirituality, as starting point and
    matrix of, xi, 8, 11, 12–13, 15, 18,
    30–31, 59, 75, 88, 102, 125, 126
spontaneous participation in, 8, 77,
    124, 130
standards of excellence for, 73, 76,
    119–22, 130
as suffused with Black culture, 13,
    15, 23, 110, 116, 119, 122, 126

tensions within, xii, 14, 19, 27, 32,
33, 39, 41–47, 48, 50–51, 67, 80,
90, 124
tradition and creativity in, xi, 10, 23,
31, 33, 37–38, 40, 42, 44, 48,
66–67, 72, 79, 80–81, 94, 106,
116, 130
and transcendence, 52, 71, 76, 77,
121
white response to, 16, 21, 32, 76, 80
Word of God as central to, 21, 57,
63–64, 72, 75, 76, 90, 91, 111, 112,
113, 120, 126
See also liturgical arts; liturgical
innovations; liturgical music
African American Catholics
attracted to Catholic church/
worship, 4, 21
empowerment, agency of, xii, 62,
138 (n.11)
evangelization of and by, 17–18,
23–24, 34, 92, 93
finding a home in the church, 10,
18, 20, 25–26, 37, 46
frustration, marginalization of, 4,
92, 117–18
functional separatism of, 16
history of, xi, xiv, 3–4, 13, 15, 24, 26,
40, 94, 95, 96, 108, 118, 125, 126
indigenous leadership of, 19, 29, 33
and risk of separation, 16, 28–30, 36
ritual heritage of, 6, 9, 47
struggle for social justice by, 4, 14,
15, 16, 62, 74, 89, 92, 101, 112, 121
two religious patrimonies of, 4–5,
29, 34, 45, 50–51

African American Christianity, 5, 48,
58
See also Black Church
African American Civil Rights movement, ix, 3, 5–6, 8, 10, 11, 26, 49,
65
African American culture, 23, 56, 59,
94, 110, 117, 126
Blackness as self-identification in,
xi, xv, 4–5, 7, 17, 19, 25, 49–50,
78, 80, 107, 109, 127, 133
values of, 14, 25, 33, 95–99, 101, 109
distinctiveness of, 13, 18, 88
as diverse and dynamic, 10, 30
folklore, music, poetry, and art in, 7,
9, 13, 24, 25, 69, 74, 75, 76, 77,
93, 127
myth of racial inferiority about, 117,
118
African American experience. *See*
Black experience
African American liturgical music. *See*
liturgical music
African American prayer traditions, 8,
14, 19, 40, 56, 76
See also Black Church worship
African American religious culture, x,
48, 55, 56–57, 63, 81, 106, 116,
117, 125, 131
African American spirituality
characteristics of, 18, 30, 102
intuitive and emotive base of, 19, 30,
63, 97
African cultures
European perceptions of, 117–18
African religion, traditional, 58, 118,

African spirituality
  and sacred cosmos, 4, 30
  and sacramental worldview, 60–61
Africentricity, 29, 39–41
ancestors, honoring and libations, 4, 40
Asante, Molefi, 39

biblical pneumatology, 58–60
bishops. *See* African American Catholic Bishops; U. S. Catholic Bishops
Black Catholic Bishops. *See* African American Catholic Bishops
Black Catholic Clergy, Sisters, and Seminarians, Joint Conference, 26
Black Catholic Hymnal, 23
Black Catholic lay congresses, 4, 9, 16
Black Catholic Movement, Black Catholic liturgical movement, 7, 8–10, 15, 25, 32
Black Catholic Rite. *See* African American Catholic Rite
Black Catholic Theological Symposium (1978), xiv, 15, 87–124
Black Catholic worship. *See* African American Catholic worship
Black Church, xiv–xv, 12, 56, 58–60, 62, 64, 65, 69, 75, 95, 105, 107, 110, 111, 118, 122, 127
  Black Church worship, 13–14, 59, 62, 73, 75–77, 111–12, 116
Black culture. *See* African American culture
Black experience, 14, 24, 90–94, 95–106, 108–16, 126, 129

and divine revelation, 24, 91–95, 125
and value-formation, 95–106
Black Liturgy Subcommittee, 22, 30
Black spirituality. *See* African American spirituality
Black theology, 9, 24, 89, 92–93, 104–6, 108
Black worship. *See* African American Catholic worship; Black Church worship
Bowman, Thea, F.S.P.A., 11, 21, 25, 29, 102
Braxton, Edward Kenneth, xiv, 27–28, 87, 95–106, 126–31
Brown, Joseph A., S.J., 46

catechesis, 23, 24, 39, 41, 89, 90–95, 122, 127
  Black symbols in, 92
  as faith formation for mature faith, 92–93
  indigenization of, 91
  and liturgy, 90–96
  tradition as liberative in, 94–95
catharsis, 70–71, 73
Cone, James, 62
conversion, 57, 103–4, 111, 128
Conwill, Giles, 25
Copeland, M. Shawn, 5, 10, 23
creation, as inherently good, 60–61
Crollius, Ary Roest, 32–33

Davis, Cyprian, O.S.B., xiv, 3, 102
Dje Dje, Jacqueline, 12

effective worship, 55–81
eucharistic prayer texts. *See* African American Catholic worship

emotion, 31, 63–64, 68–71
  as basis of communion, 63–64
  as mystical participation, 63
  as way of knowing/learning, 31,
    63–64, 68–71
Eugene, Toinette, xiv, 24, 64, 87,
  90–95

Fire in the Pews (1987), 20–22
Freeing the Spirit, 9, 56

Haldeman, Scott, 46–47
Hayes, Diana L., 37
Holy Spirit. *See* African American
  Catholic worship
hybridity, cultural, xi, 55

Imani Temple, 17, 26–27, 45, 46
inculturation, xii, xv, 6, 17, 22–24,
    28–51, 56, 78, 79
  Africentricity as means of, 39–41
  as interculturation, 56, 67, 71, 80
  and liberation, xii
  phases of, 32–33
*In Spirit and Truth: Black Catholic
  Reflections on the Order of Mass,*
    22–23, 30–33, 43, 49

Jean-Marie, Glenn V., xiv, 4, 15, 29, 87,
    106–16, 123–24, 126–130
Jesus Christ, 11, 32, 57–58, 59, 60, 62,
    91–94, 103, 108–9, 112, 115,
    116, 126
  and Blackness, 107
  as Emancipator, 5, 14, 62
John Paul II (pope), 7, 25

King, Dr. Martin Luther, Jr., 74, 114
Kwanzaa, and Christmastide, 40

Lead Me, Guide Me, 23
liberation, xii, 5, 10, 14, 45, 61–62, 73,
    79, 83, 92, 93, 105, 108, 113, 115,
    116, 121, 123, 130
liturgical aesthetic, African American
    Catholic, xiv, 8, 12–15, 87–130
  and aesthetic patterns of human
    experience, 100–1
  goal of, 125–26
  performative values of, 1232
  as rooted in Black history, culture,
    spirituality, sociopolitical context,
    125
liturgical arts, 8, 10, 18, 75–81
liturgical innovations, 29, 38, 40, 43,
    50
liturgical music, African American, 5,
    7–8, 9, 11–12, 13, 18, 19, 20–23,
    24, 35, 56, 59, 70, 74, 77–78, 88,
    93, 97, 107, 117–20, 126–31, 134
  African American gospel, 8, 9, 10,
    12, 23, 77, 127
  composers and musicians of, 8, 9,
    23, 28, 29, 40
  and dance, 8, 12, 21, 24, 30, 40, 56,
    59, 63, 70, 129
  and drums, piano, 8, 10
  freedom as essence of, 12, 77
  hymnody, anthems, metered music,
    11, 12, 23, 77, 127
  rhythm, improvisation in, 8, 11, 12,
    14, 18, 31, 56, 60, 61, 70, 75, 77
  spirituals, 8, 10, 11–12, 23, 30, 127

liturgical renewal, xii, 10, 11, 13, 17, 20,
    23, 50, 65, 81
    and social change, revolution, xii, 88
lived religion, x–xi
Lumas, Eva Marie, S.S.S., 24
Lyke, James, O.F.M., 14, 19–20, 24,
    29, 78
    on the state of Black Catholic
    liturgy, 19–20

McCarron, Richard, 45–46
McClain, William B., 13–14
Mitchell, Nathan D., 63
Murray, J-Glenn, S.J., 41, 44–47
music, African American liturgical.
    See liturgical music, African
    American

National Black Catholic Clergy Caucus
    (NBCCC), 6, 16, 33, 34, 35, 38,
    40
National Black Catholic Congress
    (NBCC), 17, 25, 27, 29, 34,
    35–36, 40, 48
National Office for Black Catholics
    (NOBC), 9, 13, 16
Nussbaum, Martha, 63

oral/aural culture. *See* African Amer-
    ican Catholic worship
Order of Mass, Roman Catholic. *See*
    Roman rite
orthopathy, 64

Paul VI (pope), 7, 109
Phelps, Jamie, O.P., 37
Phleger, Michael, 21

Plenty Good Room (journal), 41, 43–47
*Plenty Good Room: The Spirit and Truth
    of African American Catholic
    Worship*, 30–33, 43, 49

Raboteau, Albert, xiv
racism, and systematic cultural
    hegemony, xi, 6, 16, 38
revelation. *See* Black experience and
    revelation
Right Rites, 34, 35
Rivers, Clarence R. J., xiii, xiv, 7–15,
    55–84, 87–89, 107, 117–24,
    126–31
    on performative approach to
    worship, 56, 58–78, 79, 87–89
    on effective worship, 55–84
Roman Missal for the Dioceses of
    Zaire, The, 26, 36, 47
Roman rite, Latin rite, 19, 27, 28, 29,
    32, 33, 34, 41–50, 78, 88, 110, 122,
    130
    approved innovations as departures
    from, 47
    genius of, 68
    internal logic of, and internal logic
    of Black culture, 110, 116, 130
    limitations, untapped potential of,
    23
    structure of, 21, 46, 46, 67, 71, 129–
    130, 156 (n.60)
Rowe, Cyprian Lamar, S.M., 4, 13, 29,
    43–46

sacramental worldview, 60–61
sacramentality, 4, 13, 18, 57, 60–61,
    68, 75

sacred and secular. *See* African American Catholic worship

Scott, Leonard G., 36

Senghor, Leopold Sedar, 63, 69–70

slavery, 11, 12, 30, 37, 58, 62, 65, 77, 81, 112, 118

soul, 12, 13, 31, 58–60, 64, 73, 74, 75, 76, 77, 82–84, 100, 120, 122, 126

  as biblical legacy of all Christians, 60

  and soulful participation, 60, 64, 73, 75, 77, 122

  theology of soul, 59–60

Soulfull Worship, 12, 56

Spirit in Worship, The, 13, 56, 78, 79, 133

Stallings, George, 17, 21, 26, 27, 144 (n. 72)

Study of the Opinions of African American Catholics, A, 35–39

This Far by Faith: American Black Worship and Its African Roots, 13

Thurman, Howard, 102

Tolton, Augustus, 4

tradition, liturgical, x, xiii, 5, 23, 32, 40, 56, 66–67, 70, 114, 130

  appropriated creatively, 66–67

United States Catholic Bishops, 16, 17, 22, 25, 29, 44, 47, 49, 140 (n.15)

values, human, 97–99, 104, 126–28

  as primarily affective, 96–97

  as vital, social, cultural, personal, religious, 97–99

Vatican II, liturgical reforms, xi, 3, 5, 11, 36, 43, 47, 50, 80, 81, 109, 112

  Sacrosanctum Concilium: Constitution on the Sacred Liturgy, 36, 41, 43, 47–48, 109

  and "radical adaptation," 7, 26, 43

Varietates legitimae: Inculturation and the Roman Liturgy, 41–49

  response of African American Catholics to, 43–49

What We Have Seen and Heard, 17–19, 30

Whitt, D. Reginald, O.P., 27, 47–49

Word of God. *See* African American Catholic worship